Leadership and the City

T0330957

The twenty-first century has been dominated by an almost compulsive race to find new pathways for city development. As cities seek to regenerate via the knowledge-based economy, now more than ever dynamic leadership is required in order to navigate new and complex challenges while building community. This book is about generative leadership in knowledge city development.

Leadership and the City is rooted in a conviction that the leadership in a city is crucial in order for it to adjust strategically to major transformations and thus secure a good future for its inhabitants. The book opens a fresh view of leadership by focusing on generative leaders and their modes of leading, instead of spatial categorisations, governance structures and/or policy contents and processes. It investigates generative leadership by elaborating the modes of leadership, power and strategies in influence networks. The key points are highlighted with several empirical cases. These include Münich (Germany), Leeds (UK), Barcelona (Spain) as well as Helsinki, Tampere and Seinäjoki (Finland).

This book will be of interest to researchers and practitioners concerned with Leadership, Urban Studies and Strategic Management.

Markku Sotarauta is professor of policy-making theories and practices in the School of Management, University of Tampere, Finland.

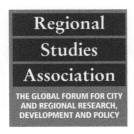

Regions and Cities
Series Editor in Chief:
Susan M. Christopherson, *Cornell University, USA*

Editors:
Maryann Feldman, *University of Georgia, US*
Gernot Grabher, *HafenCity University Hamburg, Germany*
Ron Martin, *University of Cambridge, UK*
Martin Perry, *Massey University, New Zealand*

In today's globalised, knowledge-driven and networked world, regions and cities have assumed heightened significance as the interconnected nodes of economic, social and cultural production, and as sites of new modes of economic and territorial governance and policy experimentation. This book series brings together incisive and critically engaged international and interdisciplinary research on this resurgence of regions and cities, and should be of interest to geographers, economists, sociologists, political scientists and cultural scholars, as well as to policy-makers involved in regional and urban development.

For more information on the Regional Studies Association visit www.regional studies.org

There is a **30% discount** available to RSA members on books in the ***Regions and Cities*** series, and other subject-related Taylor and Francis books and e-books including Routledge titles. To order, e-mail alex.robinson@tandf.co.uk, or phone on +44 (0) 20 7017 6924 and declare your RSA membership. You can also visit www.routledge.com and use the discount code: **RSA0901**

Leadership and the City

Power, strategy and networks in the making of knowledge cities

Markku Sotarauta

Routledge
Taylor & Francis Group

LONDON AND NEW YORK

First published 2016
by Routledge
2 Park Square, Milton Park, Abingdon, Oxon OX14 4RN

and by Routledge
711 Third Avenue, New York, NY 10017

First issued in paperback 2018

Routledge is an imprint of the Taylor & Francis Group, an informa business

British Library Cataloguing in Publication Data
A catalogue record for this book is available from the British Library

Library of Congress Cataloging in Publication Data
A catalog record for this book has been requested

ISBN 13: 978-1-138-33965-1 (pbk)
ISBN 13: 978-1-138-80406-7 (hbk)

Typeset in Times New Roman
by Florence Production Ltd, Stoodleigh, Devon, UK

For Nina

Contents

Figures

Tables

Acknowledgements

This book is embedded in my almost three decades-long effort to understand how cities and regions evolve, and what we can do to promote their economic development. Writing about it is an arduous but enjoyable experience. Arduous, since the dynamics of economic development keep changing and the more I learn, the better I understand that there is more to be learned. Enjoyable, as this field covers so much of human life and it has given me the opportunity to gain experience of exciting places all over the world, and also because there are so many people in different countries to share this endeavour with. I know that saying all this sounds clichéd; there aren't many scholarly books that would not begin like this – the thing is that it is true.

This book stems from the observation, and my personal experience, that it is always easier to identify the elements of success and/or failure in retrospect than it is to find new development paths for the future in the middle of uncertain and open-ended situations. Additionally, it is always surprising to see that in some cases leaders who possess formal power may have almost no influence at all, and to witness at close hand how actors without formal power or designation can make a difference. Conversely, it has taken me some time to see that in the development of the city, in retrospect, true leaders do not always get credit for their contributions or any acknowledgment at all, while actors who make very minor or non-existent contributions but have visible positions in the social fabric may become celebrated leaders. I have made these inescapable conclusions in the various academic leadership positions I have held and in the research projects I have been involved in, as well as through my close collaboration with many local, regional and national economic development practitioners in Finland and other countries. Indeed, a personal research strategy is never truly personal, but is collective, and thus also a book is a collective endeavour for which the author has sole responsibility.

Close collaboration with many cities and regions has led me to wonder, time after time, why, in some places, people simply are better at adjusting themselves to changing situations than in others. The answer is not always found in differing policies and structures, but in the ways resources and competencies are mobilised and coordinated. The research I have carried out for and with cities, my consultations with them and my contribution to hundreds of development workshops and seminars, as well as confidential conversations with many local and regional government chief executives, economic development officers, national level civil servants and politicians in many countries, has convinced me that in some places the actors indeed are more capable of exploiting their resources, creating new resources, exploring new opportunities and tapping into resources and knowledge external to their cities and regions than in some other places. In dynamic places actors not only talk about "networking", "strategy" and "innovation" but they actually do something to pool the dispersed resources and competencies to serve a common purpose. There are differences in leadership capacity, I have realised.

I warmly acknowledge the indirect contribution of the practitioners who have had the courage to experiment with some of my ideas and theories, and the patience to listen to the monologues (lectures and presentations) and teach me how the "world beyond theories actually functions". All of this has been a priceless experience to my efforts to theorise and conceptualise agency in urban and regional economic development. Yes, it all goes back to the theory, as it guides the thinking in the world of local and regional economic development too – it is a pity that so many of the practitioners do not realise how much the theories indirectly guide their actions, assumptions and beliefs. I have learned a lot from the practice, but I have learned even more from the many colleagues I have been working with during the past twenty years. I would like to express my gratitude to all of them, but there is space here to name only few, mainly my co-authors in the earlier attempts to make our thinking visible.

I want to express my gratitude to Richard Lester (MIT) who, in the Local Innovation Systems Project, gave me much food for thought about innovation-led local economic development trajectories and interpretive leadership, and also about how to write great books of unprecedented elegance. Unfortunately, inspiration does not always translate into quality of the same calibre. I also very much enjoyed my collaboration with Smita Srinivas. Also deserving my gratitude are John Gibney, Andrew Beer, Lummina Horlings, and Joyce Liddle as well as everybody else involved in the Regional Studies Association's research network on "Leadership in Urban and Regional Development" and "Understanding Regional Innovation Policy Dynamics: Actors, Agency and Learning". The Regional Studies Association's research networks have proved to be excellent platforms for thinking together. Most importantly, I draw extensively upon empirical observations and insights made in the European project "Secondary Cities in Territorial Development". It was the best-led project I have ever contributed to, and thus it was a great learning experience about cities in Europe and, as a by-product, about project management – thank you Michael Parkinson and the entire three-country research team. Michael Parkinson, Richard Meegan and Richard Evans also deserve warm thanks for their agreement to the inclusion of their case studies in this book.

The many projects carried out in collaboration with the super active regional innovation and knowledge dynamics community have been a platform for understanding and developing ideas concerning regional innovation systems, combinatorial knowledge dynamics and many other interesting issues. I have gained much from collaboration with Ron Boschma, Björn Asheim, Phil Cooke, Charles

Edquist, Jerker Moodysson, Arne Isaksen, James Karlsen, Robert Hassink and so many others – you know the community I refer to. David Charles deserves my gratitude for joint research, his longstanding friendship and the opportunity to spend some time at Newcastle University (UK) as a visiting professor. I want to express my thanks also to my favourite Findian, Alok Chakrabarti, for his longstanding friendship and many interesting conversations. On a more practical level, warm thanks are due to Rob Langham and Lisa Thomson at Routledge for their encouragement and advice in planning and preparing this book. You are true professionals. My academic home, the University of Tampere, is a pleasant and in many ways excellent environment for the pursuit of one's academic compulsions. My thanks to you all collectively, especially to everybody involved in the research activities of the "Urban and Regional Studies Group" (Sente) and the teaching in "Local and Regional Governance" programme.

This book brings together observations and conceptualisations from many earlier studies, and much of what is written here has already been published in one form or another earlier. This is not to say that this is a copy and paste book, since as I have been putting it together I have taken pains to throw away a lot of material, rewrite most of it and add new pieces into the broth. I am grateful to several publishers for allowing me to use previously published material. Some parts of Chapters 3 and 5 draw upon my article "Regional Development and Regional Networks: The Role of Regional Development Officers in Finland", published in *European Urban and Regional Studies* (2010). Chapters 1.3 and 8 draw partly upon an article in a book published by Ashgate and edited by Henrik Halkier and Iwona Sagan. The article was entitled "Shared Leadership and Dynamic Capabilities in Regional Development". A large part of Chapter 5 is based on the article "Power and Influence Tactics in the Promotion of Regional Development: An Empirical Analysis of the Work of Finnish Regional Development Officers", published in *Geoforum* (2009). Chapter 7 draws upon my article, co-authored by Toni Saarivirta, entitled "Strategy Development in Knowledge Cities Revisited: The Roles of Innovation Strategy in Helsinki Metropolitan Area explored", published by Gower in a book edited by Hans Christian Garmann Johnsen and Richard Ennals. Most parts of Chapter 6 draw upon my earlier work for Routledge with Nina Mustikkamäki, published in the book "Leadership and Change in Sustainable Regional Development" (2012), which I coedited with Lummina Horlings and Joyce Liddle. Another piece I draw upon in Chapter 6 is from a book published by Routledge entitled *The Social Dynamics of Innovation Networks*, edited by Roel Rutten, Paul Benneworth, Dessy Irawati and Frank Boekema. My chapter was entitled "Territorial Knowledge Leadership in Policy Networks: A Peripheral Region of South Ostrobothnia, Finland as a Case in Point". As a clever reader may have already guessed, the assumption here is that not many have read all the publications mentioned above, if any of them. Moreover, it might be difficult to see that they are parts of the same two decades long endeavour.

Finally and most importantly – Nina, I know I write too much – often without any visible means. I dedicate this book to you.

1 Introduction

1.1 Beyond the spectacle of authority and happy families

This book is about generative leadership in knowledge city development. It is rooted in a conviction, albeit not proven, that the leadership in a city is crucial in order for it to adjust strategically to major transformations and thus secure a good future for its inhabitants. Generative leadership is central in these efforts, as it focuses on those processes that are geared to giving birth to something new and constructing local conditions for knowledge creation, circulation and valorisation. This is important, as the future is not something waiting somewhere around the corner only to be anticipated and planned for, but something that is with us today, that is emerging in front of us, in spite of us, or contributed to by us. All this calls for leadership, as the future needs to be discovered, created, made sense of and shaped. The more complex economic development and associated governance systems are becoming, the more city development is dependent on the capacity for leadership emerging from those cities. The main premise here is that successful efforts to boost city development depend both on the ability to exploit existing resources, and on creating and attracting new resources, and this calls for mobilisation of collective action and pooling existing and new knowledge, power and resources, to serve more or less collective purposes. This again calls for better understanding of how actors influence each other in the construction of shared strategic intentions and agreement on that which needs to be done and how.

Beer and Clower (2014) conclude their literature review on leadership in cities and regions by arguing that there is an emerging consensus among researchers, think tanks and policy-makers that "place-based leadership" is important for economic development. It is thus easy to follow Gibney (2011a; 2011b) and Collinge *et al.* (2011) who claim that leadership cannot be ignored in this context either. They base their argument upon a series of case studies that show how leadership is one of the factors that explains how some places are able to adapt to new situations, and to exploit the emerging opportunities (see also Sotarauta *et al.*, 2012). Rodríguez-Pose (2013) suggests that leadership may be the missing factor in our efforts to understand why some places grow and others do not. We need to start modestly, however, as, in spite of visible progress in understanding urban growth and change, we are still far from identifying the causes of change processes (Storper, 2013), not to mention the role of leadership. As Storper

(2013: 4–5) points out, the problem is that "we still mostly account for patterns in a *post hoc* manner, or attribute causes to them by oversimplifying, thus bracketing out most of the interesting interactions". Of course, as Storper also states, the economic development of cities is shaped by an almost infinite set of socio-politico-economic forces. It is more or less an impossible task to study all these forces in full.

Additionally, there is a need to be aware of the main traps in any place leadership study. These kinds of studies may be compromised by retrospective analyses that introduce causal links between improved performance and skilful leadership practices. This again may lead to overly simplistic "happy family stories" assuming that micro-level practices might cause better local and/or regional performance more or less automatically (Benneworth, 2004; Lagendijk and Oinas, 2005; Benneworth *et al.*, 2010; Benneworth *et al.*, forthcoming). It might be fair to add that other fields of interest in local and regional development studies may fall into the same trap. We should not assume that the existence of higher education institutions or regional innovation systems might cause better local performance more or less automatically either. In any case, this book aims to understand leadership in a city, and not to explain the economic performance of a city through leadership practices.

Another trap is that a strong current towards managerial approaches and a focus on people and positions of authority in corporate settings dominates leadership studies, and thus our understanding of the field. The main purpose of this book is to reach beyond, as Couto (2010: xv) so elegantly puts it, "the spectacle of authority and its assumption of hierarchy", and to find a way to understand leadership as a process of social influence in the context of knowledge city development. The spectacle of authority and hierarchy is not to be overlooked, as it exists and does well, but there is so much beyond it. This book focuses mainly on a selected group of economic development agents, those people whose job it is to promote economic development in their respective cities. Not all of them have a formal leadership position, but many need to earn a position and the respect of others in wider networks to make a difference, and their leadership is definitely beyond the spectacle of formal authority. Of course, there are also leaders who have a formal position, and who use it well to boost economic development of their cities.

1.2 Strategic intentions and emergence

It should be acknowledged at the outset that there are always conflicting reactions to leadership. It is easy to underrate its significance and argue that complex multi-actor city development is not led but is the result of many forces, and of the combined effort of all the firms, other organisations and people living in a city, or that it is impossible to identify the leaders who really make a difference. In *War and Peace*, Leo Tolstoy famously suggests that leaders are mere figureheads, and are controlled by events rather than vice versa. We might say the same thing about contemporary city mothers and fathers, and not only about leaders in the early nineteenth-century Napoleonic Wars. In the words of Uyarra (2010), an urban and regional development is "truly a product of particular time-space contexts and thus an outcome of "an emergent property" of contingent historical processes". Tolstoy's and Uyarra's views do not suggest that leadership does not play any role at all, but they raise the question of what the role of leadership actually is in the big picture of continuously evolving events that again are the sum of an endless series of individual and group level efforts. We follow here Grint's (2001) proposition that while the role of individual leaders may be limited, the significance of leader*ship* ought not to be underestimated. We also follow Samuels (2003), who says that leaders are more than "vessels for irresistible and inevitable change", and by their own choices and actions stretch the many constraints that shape the course of events, and thus they may significantly influence how the future emerges. The view proposed here does not subscribe to those views that argue individual local leaders as mere pawns in the hands of the masses and market forces.

As easy as it is to overemphasise grand societal and economic forces over leaders, it would also be to overemphasise the role of individuals by giving some visible leader(s) all the credit. We often mystify leadership and reconstruct the notion of a leader as a talented, visionary and strong person who controls and provides their followers with a visionary direction. This book positions itself somewhere in between the Tolstoyan notion of leadership as rule of the masses, and those elite theorists who argue that all political structures will inevitably be dominated by small groups of office holders (Elcock, 2001) who might traditionally be labelled as strong leaders. In practice, the forms of power are many, and thus the question of what "strong leader" refers to may also have many forms of manifestation.

Aiming to influence the course of events, leaders are pinched by the strategic intentions of many actors, but also by a series of emergent forces that are beyond their control. The idea of "emergence" directs our attention to such qualities that appear "from nowhere" as a result of the many intertwined processes of many single organisations and individuals; quite often it seems as if "things simply happen" (Johnson, 2002). Emergent properties or qualities are by their very nature unpredictable; they cannot be predicted or envisioned from the knowledge we possess at a given time. As Alchian (1950: 214) says, uncertainty and chance are incorporated in this thinking: "sheer chance is a substantial element in determining the situation selected and also in determining its appropriateness or viability". More specifically, emergence can be defined as an overall system of behaviour that comes from the interaction of many participants, and cannot be predicted or even envisioned from the knowledge of what each component of a system does in isolation (Holland, 1995). An emergent system, as a whole, develops organically and without any predestined goals, even though their elements, organisations and individuals have explicit goals to pursue. Emergence is an order that arises out of complex dynamic systems, in which an understanding of the interaction of "the whole" and "the parts" is essential. Some kind of larger property emerges from the interaction of the individual components, the qualities of the whole, something that is impossible to predict from what is known of the parts (Lewin,

1993). The emergent behaviour feeds back to influence the behaviour of individuals and local interactions. Quite often it is seen that both organisations and individuals act within an overall framework of the emergent whole, and they adapt and design strategies within it – that is exactly where local generative leadership has a chance to nudge development in desired directions. A city, beyond any doubt, is an emergent system.

Emergence stresses the fact that the institutional structure is actually produced by local interaction and thus agents at the same time construct their environment and adapt to it (Lewin, 1993; Sotarauta and Srinivas, 2006). In this kind of complex and evolutionary understanding of economic development, it is not possible for actors to fully analyse their own situation or the environment, and based on those analyses to design optimal strategy. This does not mean that agents cannot direct their own actions, shape the city and influence the course of events; they can, but they always face constraints and surprises. As Axelrod (1997) states, actors reconcile their strategies with those strategies that have been successful in the past, and to what and how the other agents are doing. They also reconcile their actions with their future expectations and selection environment (for more about strategic agency, see Lagendijk, 2007). By necessity, most selection events, as well as successful development strategies can only be recognised as such after the fact. The influence of individual agents is, of course, minor, but for generative leadership emergence opens up fresh insights into economic development.

Many of the policy-oriented urban and regional development studies do not recognise confusion, ignorance and chance associated with leadership, as forces causing and directing development, explicitly enough. In practice, any effort to boost economic development in cities consists of people who do not always know what it is that they do not know, and therefore they do not know how they will react when they do know "it" (Allen, 1990). Usually this kind of uncertainty and ambiguity is seen as something that needs to be removed by skilful analysis, management and planning. In generative leadership, ambiguity is seen as a source of innovation and development. In this thinking, the past provides systems with a range of possible states of the present, and in a way the strategic choices are made in the interplay of actors and surprises emerging from the operational environment (Sotarauta and Srinivas, 2006). If cities are seen as systems that are nexuses and platforms of the many co-evolutionary processes between intention and emergence, then it may be possible to develop a new understanding of intentionality and the role of leadership in the economic development of cities.

If emergence is taken seriously, it suggests that the economic development of cities is an uncontrolled process and the policy-makers and various development officers should not pretend otherwise, but, quite naturally, many scholars and practitioners alike stress teleological explanations, and the importance of shared purpose, consensus and cooperation are thus stressed as important factors in pursuing change. These views are often well argued from their own points of departure, but they seldom acknowledge emergence as an important factor. Instead of prescriptively stating, for example, that innovation systems and the interaction of academia, firms and the public sector are needed for knowledge city development, it is stressed here that there is a need to better understand the co-evolution of emergence and intentionality and, based on that, improve our abilities to intentionally direct constantly evolving processes. Intention refers to a direction of thinking, decisions and actions that are settled toward selected acts. Actors with intention are thus resolved and determined to do something and expose their willingness to act to other actors. Intentions become strategic when they address the crucial issues of city development in the long run and when they focus on the creation of a new space that is uniquely suited to the city's needs; space that is not on the traditional map. Strategic intention, therefore, refers to a determination of generative leadership to act in a certain way for the long-term development of a city. The main motive in generative leadership is not to find the best fit between existing resources and current opportunities, but to create a misfit between resources and ambitions, to challenge the actors to join development efforts.

Strategic intention is a manifestation of (a) imaginable and desirable future states; (b) desired accomplishments; (c) the position of generative leadership in wider governance systems; and (d) the establishment of criteria to judge progress (see for more in detail, Chapter 7). All this suggests that the relationship between strategic intentions and emergence is not reactively but strategically and dynamically adaptive. In this kind of strategic adaptation, both adaptation to the changing environment and the strategic choices and intentions of actors play a significant role. Strategic adaptation in general endows a city with the capacity to change its destiny by adapting itself to changes and reshaping its local selection environments. This approach emphasises the strategic intentionality to function as an intermediary between a city and its environment. It is often reflected in new or restructured institutions, interpretations and abilities (Sotarauta and Srinivas, 2006).

From the premises set in this chapter, generative leadership is needed for (a) bringing something new into being, and creating proper conditions for novelty, and for this purpose, generative leaders (b) construct collective intentions and strategies to promote the economic development of a city, (c) take advantage of emergent developments and minimise their side effects, and (d) launch new development processes and shepherd them to execution – and all this in a city development world that is genuinely shaped by both many intentions and emergent forces, as explained by a senior official from a Finnish ministry.

[Y]ou have to understand that this not a positivistic world. It is no longer about the world of planning or engineering where A leads to B and then to C. This is a genuinely continuous hustle and bustle and you can't always know what depends on what, what measures lead where. Understanding this fuzzy logic is not important as such; you can't understand it, you just have to accept it – to accept that many of these processes simply are ambiguous and fuzzy. You need to experiment with some paths to take, and see if they're ok; if you find a good one, you then move on but you need to have several options up your sleeve all the time.

1.3 Main schools of thought and basic definitions of leadership

Leadership is an intriguing subject of study. More or less all of us have some under-standing of what it is, and it might be safe to argue that many of us have complained about bad leadership or lack of it at some point of our lives. Conversely, sometimes we may raise a hero on a podium, and praise their vision and abilities. As Northouse (2007) says, leadership is a highly sought-after and valued commodity, as we tend to believe that it secures good futures not only for our organisations and communities but also ourselves. Sometimes this is the case, sometimes something very different happens. Skilled leaders do not always produce good results, and may use their skills for ethically or morally questionable efforts (Kellerman, 2004; Pelletier, 2010). Among many other motivations to study leadership, we should not neglect the need to identify bad leadership practices. Without understanding leadership processes, practices and structures, we would be unable to detect "good" or "bad" leadership. In spite of great efforts to discover the secrets of leadership, we need more, as times change, and different contexts call for nuanced views of the subject. This chapter is dedicated to taking a quick stock of what leadership studies say about their targets of interest and main conceptualisations.

A brief scrutiny of the root definition of leadership is begun by considering the ultimate simplification of any concept, a dictionary. By using Webster's dictionary, it is possible to say that "to lead" means (a) to go before or to show the way; (b) to influence or to induce; (c) to go at the head of or in advance of; (d) to have the advantage over; (e) to act as leader of; (f) to go through or pass; and (g) to act as a guide. All these verbs indicate that leadership is about action and not position. They may mean very different things in different times and places. As Heifetz (2010) maintains, previously formed perspectives and cultural assumptions of leadership shape our understanding of it, and thus cause confusion, sometimes also failure, as the prevailing conceptions are stronger than theories or research results. He sees the main sources of confusion where people conflate leadership with formal and informal authority, treat adaptive (or transformative) challenges as if they were technical problems, confuse managerial expertise with leadership, view leadership as a set of personal characteristics rather than set of activities, or define leadership as a value-free practice (Heifetz, 2010). Clarifying these overlapping sources of confusion in the context of city development, we continue by (briefly) exploring the main theories and definitions often found in the leadership literature. We then dig a bit deeper into the findings of governance, policy network and place leadership studies, before focusing in more detail on generative leadership.

The extensive body of leadership studies show that leadership, in addition to being context-dependent, is also a sophisticated and complex art, rather than a straightforward managerial act (Grint, 1997). Consequently, there are many ways to define leadership, and thus also several schools of thought. Leadership scholars base their definitions of leadership on the nature of influence and the role of individuals who are defined as leaders. They define leadership in terms of group processes, traits, and behaviours, or as an instrument for achieving goals (see Bass and Bass, 2008 for a detailed review). Leadership has also been studied from power relationship, transformational process and ability perspectives (Northouse, 2007, Bass and Bass, 2008). According to Komives and Dugan (2010), contemporary theories see leadership as a dynamic and reciprocal process between people who pursue common goals in a value based and complex process that is directed towards the achievement of common good through shared goals. It is fairly common to highlight the common good and social responsibility also in corporate settings. The contemporary schools of thought include transforming leadership theories, relational, collaborative and shared leadership theories, complexity leadership theories, trait and behavioural leadership theories, and industrial leadership theories.

- **Transforming leadership** theories focus on individualised consideration, intellectual stimulation, inspirational motivation and idealised influence (Bass and Riggio, 2006; Yukl, 1999).
- **Relational, collaborative and shared leadership theories approach leadership as a process,** and study it as a non-positional phenomenon. These theories revolve around ideas of participation and involvement, and the ways leaders take input from other actors. They build on the reciprocal nature of interdependent relationships, and thus also value trust and integrity (Uhl-Bien, 2006; Komives and Dugan, 2010).
- **Complexity leadership** is built upon complexity science. It conceptualises leadership as a complex dynamic process resulting from the collective need for change that emerges from the interaction of various actors. Complexity leadership focuses on systemic adaptive outcomes more than the other main approaches (Uhl-Bien *et al.*, 2007; Termeer and Nooteboom, 2012).
- **Trait and behavioural theories** (dominant in the early phases of leadership scholarship) have re-emerged with new emphasis. If the earlier studies stressed intelligence, masculinity and dominance, the contemporary generation puts more emphasis on honesty, integrity and self-confidence. The new strand of trait and behavioural studies are more interested in determining what characteristics, capacities and behaviours are essential in effective leadership (Komives and Dugan, 2010).
- **Situational and contingency theories** focus on contextual factors that may determine leadership styles in different environs. These include the path-goal theory and the leader-member-exchange–theory (LMX) under the rubric of industrial theories (see Graen and Uhl-Bien, 1995) that also are under reconceptualisation (Komives and Dugan, 2010). Broadly speaking, these theories are productivity centred and as such more leader-centric than the other theories introduced here, and more often than not they see followers as collectives rather than individual actors with specific needs (Komives and Dugan, 2010).

Looking at leadership through a structuration lens Giddens (1984) sees leaders as "knowledgeable agents" who are able to lead because they have not only the ability of reflexive monitoring but also have easier access to and/or a better command of organisational or other resources. These may include public funding or a mandate to act as a leader. Senge (1990) adds that leaders are responsible for building organisations in which people continually expand their ability to understand complexity, clarify vision and improve shared mental models. Leaders are responsible for collective learning (Senge, 1990), and particularly for choreographing and directing learning processes among their followers. Bennis (1999) says that leadership is a function of having a vision that is well communicated, building trust, and taking effective action to realise one's own leadership potential (Bennis, 1999). Heifetz (1994) notes that a major challenge of leadership is to draw attention and then deflect it to the questions and issues that need to be faced. To do this, one has to provide context for the action and a story line that gives meaning to action. Followers need to comprehend the purpose of adaptive or transformative measures so that they focus less on the person and more on the meaning of the new action, and thus they need to be actively involved in the sense-making process.

As the heart of leadership goes beyond issues of authority, its essence is found in the question of "how individuals or groups can take action to mobilise adaptive work in their communities so that they can thrive in a changing and challenging work" (Heifetz, 2010). Interestingly, Heifetz links leadership conceptually to adaptation, which in his view refers to successfully taking the best of a community's history into the future. In contrast, he sees management "as the activity of coordinating complex systems in the efficient production of solutions to routine or technical problems" (Heifetz, 2010). Heifetz (1994) sees leadership both as conservative and progressive. His view of leadership serves generative leadership well, as it links leadership conceptually with the concept of strategic adaptation. What seems to be critical in Heifetz's view is whether leaders have the ability to influence people when there is a need to reach beyond routine, and when one cannot only rely on past experience. Many of the main contemporary theories also remind leaders to reflect situations and challenges back towards their followers, and to search for solutions in close interaction with them.

While there often is disagreement about the constitution of good leadership, there is widespread agreement on the importance of (a) the personal qualities of an individual leader (e.g., commitment, energy, vision) and (b) the context (an effective approach to leadership in one setting might not be appropriate in another) (Hambleton, 2003; Hambleton and Sweeting, 2004). The main theories of leadership help us to understand the spectrum of approaches and assumptions in the field. As the definitions of some of the lead authorities show, regardless of the theory they draw upon, leadership definitions revolve around such concepts as influence and power, groups of actors, followers, goals, movement and direction, process, mobilisation and access to resources.

The leader is someone who has followers.

(Drucker, 1998)

Leadership is a process whereby an individual influences a group of individuals to achieve a common goal.

(Northouse, 2007)

Organisational and political activity become leadership only when people take action mobilising other actors to tackle tough, collective problems, get work done, and generate adaptive solutions.

(Heifetz, 1994)

Leaders are actors who have a greater range of assets than others in the community for stretching the constraints.

(Samuels, 2003)

Leadership is closely related to movement – that is, getting a body of followers to move in one direction or another.

(Grint, 2001)

Effective leadership is not about making speeches or being liked; leadership is defined by results and not by attributes.

(Drucker, 1998)

Leaders are those actors who more than others influence social activities and relationships towards the production, reproduction or transformation of a social order.

(Bass, 1991)

In a search for the nature of leadership in the context of the economic development of cities, above definitions raise a series of intriguing questions: what is it to actually lead the complex, ambiguous and muddled process of city development? How is it possible to go before or to induce or to act as a guide if one does not have formal power to do it? How is it possible to take the lead, if one is assigned but not respected? How is it possible to create a vision that gives direction to whole communities, how is it possible to get people excited, how is it possible to mobilise people?

1.4 The purpose of the book

The critical issue of how leadership can be exercised to nurture strategic adaptation, innovation and high renewal capacity is insufficiently emphasised in the local and regional economic development literature. Leadership is conventionally seen as a formally constituted hierarchical power, but for knowledge city development it needs to be rethought. The main purpose of this book is to open an alternative view of leadership by focusing on generative leaders and their modes of leading, instead of spatial categorisations, governance structures and/or policy contents and processes. We set out to investigate what generative leadership is, and how it is exercised in a complex, interdependent world of knowledge city development. Consequently, the aim is to flesh out how generative leaders may give birth to new structures and processes that enable cities to reinvent themselves. This book is rooted in a belief that city development is a neverending interplay between individual and collective intentions on the one hand, and strategic intentions and emergence on the other (see also Sotarauta and Mustikkamäki, 2012).

Multi-actor forms of strategy and policy-making challenge the straightforward definitions of any development strategy that see it as something the public sector performs alone and that flows from planning to decision-making to implementation. Knowledge city strategy is comprehended here as a multiagent, multiobjective, multivision and pluralistic process, in which the actual lines of action are shaped continuously. In this kind of policy world, political and economic pressures and differing interests are an essential part of efforts to develop a city, and this is exactly why leadership is called for, and why by studying it we might learn something new about city development. Leadership is approached as a collaborative advantage (Trickett and Lee, 2010; Garman Johnsen and Ennals, 2012) that is difficult to achieve. Consequently, there is a need to study self-reflexive individuals more deeply by looking at "the process of organising/instituting as it unfolds, and on the influences and implications of such organising/instituting" (Amin 2001: 1240). As Philo and Parr (2000) say, however, the spidery networks of dispersed intentions, resources, power and abundant sources of knowledge in particular institutional geographies, for some reason, loom in the shadows of urban and regional development studies, somewhere behind structural issues. Perhaps power and leadership are not important after all or, more likely, they are so important that we do not dare to touch them. At all events, generative leadership is approached as a force to mobilise, coordinate and direct evolving processes in desired directions, and for their construction in the first place. At its best, generative leadership can serve city development as a nexus of intention and emergence, as well as the sets of individual intentions of individual actors. As city development is concerned with long-term processes, leadership is also seen as a force in time rather than a leader–follower relationship in the here and now. Leadership requires a temporally sensitive conceptualisation, and for that purpose the concept of generative leadership relay is introduced in Chapter 6.

For obvious reasons, this book does not aim to find causality between leadership and economic development; it is way too early to even make an effort. We might end up searching for causality between what we see, formal leadership and GDP growth, for example, instead of identifying the true nature and nuances of generative leadership. In the knowledge-based economic development of cities, and such closely related issues as cluster development and regional innovation systems, leadership has hardly been studied at all, not least as these entities have been somewhat carelessly labelled as self-organising entities without proper consideration of agency (Sydow *et al.*, 2011; Uyarra, 2010) not to mention leadership. As Beer and Clower (2014) note, the analytical challenge is to better understand leadership in urban and regional development, as it is different by nature from conventional bureaucratic organisations such as company, public organisation or city administration. The kind of approach proposed in this book might provide us with a more sensitive view of the complexities of city development, and thus also of such often-used concepts as strategy, power and network. In our efforts to unravel the noisy and complex problem of the forward-moving development of cities, additional analytical leverage might be gained by adding leadership approaches and research tools to our research agenda.

This book sets out to search for the nature of leadership in cities by keeping three perspectives in mind: (a) the *process* perspective that informs a study on dynamism and secures a temporally conscious approach, (b) the *network* perspective that informs about the social relationships of actors beyond organisations, and (c) the *governance* perspective that informs about the wider systemic issues framing and moulding both the actual systems and the development journeys as well as forms of leadership. The book probes the edges of generative leadership by presenting views yet to be tested by empirical research. The empirical cases highlight specific development processes and the leadership within them, instead of aiming to prove the theory. The main objective is to construct a conceptual framework that adds analytical leverage to our efforts to understand leadership in the economic development of cities, and more precisely:

• to construct a theoretically informed but practically rooted place for generative leadership in the promotion of knowledge-based development of cities;
• to construct a dynamic model of generative leadership that provides local and regional development scholars and practitioners with a conceptual framework by which to understand and explain the role of agency in city development;
• to find out how actors lead complex networks of knowledge-based economic development; and
• to find out how key actors aim to do what they feel needs to be done, how they establish new governance and power systems, how they deploy the existing systems of power and governance as resources in their endeavours, and what kind of power they have and how they exercise influence?

To address these questions this book is built on three distinct bodies of literature: (a) local and regional economic development literature with an explicit focus on "place leadership", (b) governance and policy networks, and (c) management and organisation studies on leadership and strategy. The key rationale in bringing these three fairly disconnected bodies of literature together is that there is much to be learned across these broad fields of knowledge. This endeavour is therefore synthetic in nature.

The book discusses knowledge-based economic development as a development game, where conditions for new creations of economic, ecological and/or social significance (innovation) are consciously sought and constructed. We follow Rafiqui (2009) who makes a distinction between the spheres of beliefs (game sense), institutions (formal and informal rules of the game), strategies (ways of playing the game) and actors (players of the game). This book focuses especially on the game sense and ways of playing the games. It adds the concept of governance (playing field) in the metaphoric discussion. Leaders are influential players, who aim to change the ways games are played, playing fields and rules as well as teams. In a policy context, "game" is easily seen as a negative concept, but here it is simply a tool to illustrate various dimensions of leadership and help in clarifying complex reasoning. "Game" refers to a series of moves (actions and decisions) and countermoves in a certain context (Karppi, 1996). The game of knowledge city development refers to all those actions and decisions by the many actors who have an effect on the unfolding knowledge-based future of a city. There is not one single game, but many sub-games unfolding all the time, and thus there are numerous players in several fields who monitor each other's moves when deciding about moves of their own. Games are full of choices and situations in which there are no turns for making a move (Karppi, 1996; Sotarauta, 1997). As Karppi maintains, the details of such games have been left deliberately vague, but the message is that it is not always the measure on which a move is made that counts, but rather who makes it and in what connection (Karppi, 1996). The game of knowledge city development contains two separate but highly interlinked games: (a) the competition between cities as to which are to succeed in the future, and (b) the competition within cities concerning which groups are best able to shape their respective cities. The aim is not to cover all possible city development games but focus mainly on those games that are somehow related to knowledge city development. The metaphor of game is not used extensively but very lightly here and there. At all events, the numerous games played in cities are the soil wherein city futures are growing.

The book revolves around the concepts of generative leadership, governance, power, strategy, influence network, strategic intention and emergence (Figure 1.1). As mentioned earlier, cities ought to find strategies that enable them to shape their own futures, to adapt strategically. Strategic adaptation refers to the sensitivity to recognise various changes and to adapt to them, not like driftwood in a stream, but with purpose (Sotarauta and Srinivas, 2006). This again calls for collective strategic intentions that are channelled into action through influence networks. The course of events surprises us whatever we do, and emergence is the basic feature

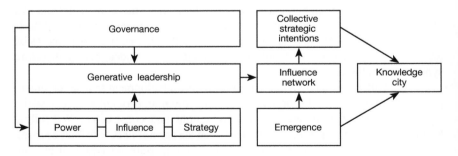

Figure 1.1 The outline of the book, the conceptual link between knowledge city development and generative leadership

of the city development. It cannot be overlooked. Emergence thus influences both influence networks and knowledge city development, and it is believed here that generative leadership is the nexus between intention and emergence, as well as many intentions.

1.5 The plan for the book

Chapter 2 sets the scene for a scrutiny of generative leadership by taking quick stock of the literature on the knowledge-based development of cities. A short scrutiny of the main concepts and development models is illustrated with a few selected cases. Chapter 3 moves the discussion to the concept of governance that is a playground of generative leadership and knowledge city games. In a way, it sets the systemic tone for the examination of leadership and the city. Chapter 3 also picks up the concept of an influence network, as it provides the discussion with a point of departure to approach leadership as a multi-actor process in which the policy content is affected by many actors and several levels of action. An influence network is seen as the main operating environment for generative leaders to influence city development. It also serves as a conceptual tool to narrow down the vast spectre of actors influencing knowledge city development by focusing the discussion mainly on conscious efforts to make a difference. As actors are mutually dependent, development strategies are both formulated and implemented in the interaction of many actors, and therefore, in order to function effectively, influence networks call for leadership.

Chapter 4 turns our attention to the concept of place leadership that provides us with the basic view of territorially-oriented forms of leadership. For its part, Chapter 5 sets out to investigate what kind of power leaders use in their efforts to influence city development through influence networks. The chapter follows Flyvbjerg's (1998) "strategic-and-tactics approach", which challenges "who governs" (Dahl, 2005) oriented studies that commonly see power as an entity. The chapter discusses the many nuances of power and the spectrum of leadership styles used by generative leaders. Chapter 6 begins by arguing that, in knowledge city development, strategy and strategic planning are often seen as direct guidance for various actors, but, as is shown, the intended strategy, the plan itself, can also be approached as an arena of struggle, with different interests competing to determine its content and ways of implementation. In a way, a "knowledge city strategy" is a sequence of choices made by many independent actors and a collective strategy process can be seen as a quest for strategic collaboration and belief formation. Consequently, there is a need to acknowledge that strategy development is not about plan making but something leaders can use in stabilising the power relations between the actors and/or a tool for including/excluding some of the actors, and a means to learn shared vocabulary for collective efforts. Therefore, this chapter suggests that strategic planning ought to be approached from the point of view of leadership instead that of plan making.

The book is conceptual by nature but the conceptual discussion is illustrated, and its key points highlighted, with several empirical cases. Our research in Finland,

and experience gained from collaboration with many Finnish cities, regions and national development bodies has strongly influenced the thinking behind this book. The main Finnish case cities are Tampere, Seinäjoki and Helsinki. Tampere serves this book as an "anchor case" that is used to highlight several different aspects of generative leadership. Tampere is used more than other cities, as it is one of those ordinary European cities that is constantly struggling to redefine itself, and, of course, as the home of the author of this book, it has been studied more from the perspectives relevant here than any other city. In addition to the Finnish cases, other cities are used to discuss the differences and similarities in leadership and development strategies. These cities include Akron and Rochester (USA), Münich (Germany), Leeds (UK) and Barcelona (Spain). The cases are not supposed to provide empirical evidence for the entire conceptual framework presented but to illustrate some aspects of it. The cases are discussed throughout the book, some more, some less. In the end, the hope is to emerge with a fuller and more nuanced view of generative leadership in a city, as well as of the interaction between leadership, power, strategy and networks, than at the outset.

The main body of case narratives is based on several empirical studies focusing on agency in urban and regional economic development, each in its own way. The most important ones are: "Secondary Cities in Territorial Development", led by the European Institute of Urban Affairs (Liverpool), and partnered by the Hungarian and Finnish teams (the Finnish team lead by the author); the "Organisational Change for Innovation and Institutional Entrepreneurship" consortium led by the author of this book and partnered by two other Nordic teams; "Local Innovation Systems" led by MIT/IPC and partnered by four other teams from Norway, England, Japan and Finland (the Finnish team led by the author); "Constructing Regional Advantage: Towards State-of-the-art Regional Innovation System Policies in Europe", which was coordinated by the University of Lund, Circle and partnered by seven European research teams (the Finnish team led by the author); "In Search of Process Based Regional Development Policy in the Nordic countries" led by the author and partnered by a team from the Helsinki University of Technology; and "Innovation Capabilities of Innovation Developers" which focused on local and regional economic development champions in Finland. In these studies, thousands of interviews were carried out and extensive statistical and secondary data was collected and analysed. The above-mentioned studies did not explicitly focus on leadership in urban and regional development, but all of them, in one way or another, ended up revolving to some extent around it, and the "Innovation Capabilities of Innovation Developers" project was designed to focus on nothing but leadership with 41 interviews and 531 respondents to a survey in Finland. This book is not a direct outcome of these research projects but is highly influenced by them, and draws upon their data as well as scientific and policy oriented conversations. All the quotes used to highlight the discussion are drawn from the Finnish interview data. They are aimed at bringing the voice of generative leaders in an otherwise fairly conceptual discussion, as the entire books aims at bringing people back to the debate. Leadership is essentially about the ways players influence the games. In the words of two Finnish generative leaders from two city governments:

> The system functions well as long as there are drivers embedded in it that motivate people. That is what's crucial, what motivates organisations and human beings to do their best.

> There are individuals who accomplish more in a month than somebody else in five years. If we do not have capable individuals here, we can forget all the strategies and other formal stuff.

2 Knowledge-based development of cities

2.1 Shared enthusiasm and a few illustrative cases

The early 21st century is dominated by an almost compulsive race to find new pathways for city development. In twenty years we have witnessed a rapid flow of key ideas and concepts ranging, back and forth, from innovative cities (Simmie, 2003) to learning cities (Campbell, 2009) to creative cities (Scott, 2006) to knowledge cities (Carrillo, 2006) to resilient cities (Vale and Campanella, 2005) to smart cities (Hollands, 2008). Many cities have been changing according to these lines, and many local leaders have found new food for thought. However, at times, the new economic development strategies seem to range from pure rhetorical gimmicks to dynamic action, and it is often difficult to distinguish these two extremes. In this book, the "knowledge city" is used as a generic metaphor that describes the overall trend in the direction many cities are attempting to develop themselves. "City" refers here simply to an urban unit within administrative borders, while the concept of a city-region links a core city by functional ties to its hinterland. Functional ties generally include a combination of economic, housing market, travel-to-work, marketing, or retail catchment factors (Rodríguez-Pose, 2008). Depending on the governance system, a city-region may or may not have a shared administrative body. "City-region" is not a homogenous entity, or concept, with clear boundaries. This book does not aim to cover leadership in a city or city-region in its entirety but deals mainly with issues related to knowledge economy and development.

Using knowledge as a component of economic development is not a totally new idea. Joseph Schumpeter is credited as first to recognise the importance of knowledge in economic development by arguing that new combinations of knowledge are at the heart of innovation and entrepreneurship (Cooke and Leyesdorf, 2006). Knowledge economies are based on following core assumptions identified by Phil Cooke: (a) knowledge quickly becomes out of date and new knowledge is constantly challenging the old, (b) scientific knowledge (including social science) is respected and permeates society faster than ever before, and (c) existing knowledge is of importance to create new knowledge (Cooke, 2002). As knowledge economy has been discussed extensively in the literature, there is no need here to engage in this debate more deeply but it is obvious that learning and knowledge creation have been strongly advocated as the principal drivers of city development. As Richard Florida wrote enthusiastically in 1995, "a new age of capitalism is sweeping the globe . . . despite continued predictions of the 'end of geography,' regions are becoming more important nodes of economic and technological organisation in this new age of global, knowledge-intensive capitalism." He described the new era as follows:

> In Silicon Valley, a global centre for new technology has emerged, where entrepreneurs and technologists from around the world backed by global venture capital invent the new technologies of software, personalised information and biotechnology that will shape our future.
>
> In the financial centres of Tokyo, New York and London, computerised financial markets provide instantaneous capital and credit to companies and entrepreneurs across the vast reaches of the world.
>
> In the film studios of Los Angeles, computer technicians work alongside actors and film directors to produce the software that will run on new generations of home electronics products produced by television and semiconductor companies in Japan and throughout Asia.
>
> Computer scientists and software engineers in Silicon Valley and Seattle work with computer game makers in Kyoto, Osaka and Tokyo to turn out dazzling new generations of high-technology computer games.
>
> In Italy, highly computerised factories produce designer fashion goods tailored to the needs of consumers in Milan, Paris, New York and Tokyo almost instantaneously.
>
> Teams of automotive designers in Los Angeles, Tokyo and Milan create designs for new generations of cars, while workers in Kyushu work to the rhythm of classical musician the world's most advanced automotive assembly factories to produce these cars for consumers across the globe.
>
> A new industrial revolution sweeps through Taiwan, Singapore, Korea, Malaysia, Thailand, Indonesia, and extends its reach to formerly undeveloped nations such as Mexico and China.
>
> And, once-written-off regions, like the former Rustbelt of the USA are being revived through international investment and the creative destruction of traditional industries.

(Florida 1995: 527–8)

This king-size quote from Richard Florida earns its place here, as it not only illustrates what the knowledge economy is all about but also the enthusiasm shared by the city and regional economic development research community and policy-makers alike. We are still on that path. Today, we perhaps do not talk as much about Japan as China, but an "industrial revolution" has truly been sweeping across the globe. We have begun to stress smart knowledge cities and their resilience. We also know much better than we did in the 1990s that this kind of transformation is not a joyride. It generates not only new industries, firms and jobs but also redundant people and skill-sets that are no longer needed. It forces many "industrial stars" of the previous era to construct new strategies for adaption. As Safford (2009) says, "the Silicon Valleys" of the Second Industrial Revolution had names like Akron, Detroit, Pittsburgh and Rochester, and in Europe we might add Manchester, Lodz, Barcelona, Tampere and many others to the list of "industrial stars". Even though we often highlight such places as Silicon Valley, Bangalore and Cambridge (UK) as shining stars of the knowledge-based third industrial revolution, some of the old industrial stars are also working hard to develop themselves and secure their place among the new era stars.

The second city-region of Finland, **Tampere** is accustomed to continuous change throughout its history. It developed first from a small village into Finland's leading industrial town (19th century) where large-scale Finnish industrialisation got under way. Today, it is quite generally acknowledged that the city-region of Tampere with its 350,000 inhabitants, is among the leading Finnish "knowledge cities", as it is the second research and development (R&D) centre in the country with a 14.5% share of national R&D spending, which in absolute terms was €1040 million in 2011 (Statistics Finland). Tampere has faced three major transformation processes in past decades. First, the textile industry declined and disappeared in the 1970s (only a few highly specialised textile firms have survived). Second, against a background of industrial recession dating back to the oil crisis of the 1970s and severe national economic recession of the early 1990s, the engineering industry succeeded in reinventing itself, renewing and developing technology of an increasingly high level. Several mergers and rearrangements of ownership took place that resulted in ownerships moving to international corporations that are among the largest in the world. Third, new and rapidly growing business sectors emerged; particularly in the 1990s, the information and telecommunications technology cluster grew rapidly, and medical technology has also been developing favourably (see Sotarauta and Srinivas, 2006; Martinez-Vela and Viljamaa, 2004; Kostiainen, 2002; Kostiainen and Sotarauta, 2003; Parkinson *et al.*, 2012; Benneworth, 2007). The transformation has indeed been visible:

> In 1960, there were approximately 33,000 industrial jobs in Tampere, which made up over 50% of all working places. That same year the first university students began their studies in Tampere. Correspondingly, in the year 2000, there were approximately 22,000 industrial jobs, which accounted for 21% of all working places in Tampere. The number of university students was about 35,000. In the span of 40 years, Tampere has transformed from the leading town of industrialised Finland into one of the foremost Finnish cities of the knowledge economy.
>
> (Kostiainen and Sotarauta, 2003: 1)

The kind of transformation Tampere has experienced includes, of course, several separate development games that have worked in the same direction, as can be seen in retrospect. In a time-span of more than forty years, the key decision-makers of Tampere have first had to deal with a lack of higher education institutions and knowledge-intensive businesses, and also the difficulties of a high unemployment rate, and other social issues caused by the economic transformations. It was not at all self-evident that Tampere, which had held a central position in industrial society, would be renewed to adapt to the knowledge economy. The continuous reinvention of the city is a story of local development policies, business sector activities and forward-looking, relatively young universities (Benneworth, 2007). As Kostiainen and Sotarauta (2003) show, the transformation was not a great leap from one era to another but a long series of critical incidents and development phases, and thus also a whole set of influential actors leading development efforts at different times.

As in Tampere, in **Akron** and **Rochester** (USA) the global competition and structural changes also lead to industrial crisis (Safford, 2009). Once Akron was known as the "tyre capital of the world", and the core of industrial concentration was formed by such prominent companies as Goodrich, Goodyear and Firestone Tire and Rubber. In Rochester, Bausch and Lomb emerged as the country's first mass-producer of eye-glasses, goggles and microscopes, and Eastman Kodak emerged as the world's leading producer of cameras and photographic film. All these firms faced fierce international competition in the 1970s and 1980s, and as a result of this thousands of production jobs were lost (Safford, 2004). As in Tampere, the crisis in Akron and Rochester as Safford (2004) show us, was also largely due to the apparent inability of companies and other organisations to innovate in a transforming economic landscape. Companies addressed this issue by acquiring portfolio companies, building new research capabilities in different areas of technology and moving some innovation activities to locations which allowed them to be more cutting edge. Community leaders responded to industrial crises with a set of new policy interventions. Policy-makers, on their part, aimed to promote conversations among firms in ways that might, as Safford states, approximate the creative cacophony that prevailed in the emerging "high-tech" hotspots. By channelling resources for research and development through universities, states hoped to build on the strong reputation of universities in the community, and their innovation-oriented resources to help upgrade innovation processes in those communities. These efforts were particularly directed at upgrading local capabilities in order to meet the requirements of increasingly demanding global markets. In general, states left it up to the universities and their potential industry partners to define exactly how this arrangement would work in practice. In fulfilling this mission, the universities as the key knowledge resources took significantly different approaches. In Akron, the university chose to bridge the structural holes, linking the research taking place in the university laboratories and the research and development laboratories of companies. In Rochester, the aim was to strengthen institutional capacity and social capital (Safford, 2004).

Barcelona, the capital city of Catalonia and the second city-region in Spain, has become one of the most celebrated European cities, as it successfully survived the massive economic transformation it has been going through during the past four decades (Marshall, 2004). Barcelona has reinvented itself, and thus it has become an example of rapid transformation from an industrial city in decline to one that has a reputation on the international market (Parkinson *et al.*, 2012). Barcelona has a long and solid tradition of classic manufacturing activities and has been the Spanish leader for many years in different production sectors that include automobiles, chemical-pharmaceutical, food, publishing, consumer electronics, etc. In recent decades, knowledge-based industries have been replacing the old industries and today, the City of Barcelona is more concentrated on services than before. Services employ more than 80% of its workers (Parkinson *et al.*, 2012). This is due to the fact that Barcelona has been able to reinvent itself by strengthening its position in Europe and attracting foreign investment, international entrepreneurs and tourists. There is no lack of writing about the reorientation of the "Barcelona model" towards a knowledge-based economy (see e.g. Marshall, 2004; Barber and Montserrat, 2010; Blanco, 2009; Pareja-Eastaway, 2009; Charnock and Ribera-Fumaz, 2011; Degen and García, 2012). There is no need to dig deeply into single cases here, but it is clear that Barcelona is also one of the examples showing that collective strategic intentions may indeed produce results.

Munich is the third largest city-region in Germany, with a population of more than two million. It is the second largest German centre for employment after Berlin. Munich is the capital of Bavaria and beyond any doubt, Munich is one of Europe's most successful second-tier cities due to its rich mix of small, medium, and large companies in a range of leading-edge sectors (automotive, ICT, banking and insurance, arts and media, armaments, biotechnology), powerful innovation system, indigenous assets, and a good quality of life (Evans, 2013). Munich is a living example of Germany's triple helix system of innovation, involving close networking and interplay between top ranked universities, many public research organisations and leading multi-national companies. Although there are some problems with unemployment and poverty, these are much less serious than in most other German cities (Parkinson *et al.*, 2012). Munich's resilience essentially stems from the complex interplay of Germany's distinctive political history and federal system. It has created a strong urban system that benefits from the established German style multi-level governance. All this supports leadership and entrepreneurialism in cities, and thus promotes Munich's inherent assets and diverse economy and the combined strength of its many knowledge institutions, innovation system and networks (Evans, 2013). The evidence suggests that historic, structural and locational factors, and agglomeration effects largely explain Munich's rise to prominence, but that sustained urban and regional leadership and effective governance and policy, especially in the technological, scientific and educational spheres coupled with intelligent urban planning, have played an increasingly important role in sustaining its competitiveness (Evans and Karecha, 2014).

Leeds is a city in northern England with a growing population of around 750,000 within its municipal boundaries, but about three million residents in the wider city-region, which comprises eleven local authorities (Gonzalez and Oosterlynck

2014). It lies at the heart of the second largest urban regional economy outside London and has grown rapidly in the last decade, owing to its strengths in commercial and financial services, higher education, administration, and medical services. In the last decades, Leeds has particularly specialised in finance-related economic activities (Gonzalez and Oosterlynck, 2014). The growth of the sector is partly due to the decentralisation of offices from London, but also the tradition of building societies in the Leeds region. Meegan (2012; 2015) says that Leeds is widely regarded as a Northern England success story for its recent growth, and that it has seen its economy evolve over time in a historical layering of investment, first in textiles, then in engineering and, most recently, in the service sectors, notably financial and business services (Meegan, 2015). Side by side with finance, property-led regeneration has been another important pillar of Leeds "skyscraper city" development strategy (Chatterton and Hodkinson, 2007).

Seinäjoki, a tiny town in Western Finland, is a case that illustrates how a geographically peripheral and small place can also successfully pursue knowledge strategies. South Ostrobothnia, the region of which Seinäjoki is the centre, has a population of 195,000, while the population of Seinäjoki Town was 60,000 in 2012. In its regional development plan of 1994, the Regional Council of South Ostrobothnia defined its weaknesses very tellingly: (a) a strong resistance to change (including Finland joining the European Union in 1995), (b) low interaction between the main organisations in the region, (c) dominance of agriculture in the regional economy, and (d) a low innovation capacity. Most of the region's firms were micro firms employing fewer than three people (e.g., furniture, farm machinery, carpet-making, and fur-farming), and most of these firms were not particularly well suited to meeting the challenges of a knowledge economy (see Harmaakorpi *et al.*, 2009). The innovation supporting structures and innovation culture were weak in the 1990s, and most of the firms were operating on short time horizons; their development and innovation activities focused mainly on pragmatic problem-solving (Harmaakorpi *et al.*, 2009). The quantity of research and development (R&D) expenditure in total was also an issue; R&D employment in the firms and public organisations, as well as the educational level, was among the lowest in Finland.

In spite of the challenges of the 1990s, 20–25 years later it can be concluded that Seinäjoki has been able to construct a local advantage by strengthening its regional innovation system and connections to the main Finnish universities and also abroad. Even the leading Finnish newspaper, *Helsingin Sanomat*, has acknowledged its promising developments. In 2010, it published an article titled "Seinäjoki is the Most Attractive: The Town has Invested Millions in Supporting Growth". The article describes how young, well-educated people have returned with their families to their home region, as there are now more opportunities for them than there once were. One of the secrets, claims the article, is that the region has invested in expertise, education, research and specialisation. It even notes that instead of a few individuals with doctoral degrees "there now are piles of them".

For its part, *Talouselämä*, one of the main business magazines, entitled an article praising Seinäjoki as "It is the Attitude that Counts, Proves Seinäjoki". The article concludes that instead of becoming a showcase for low-tech Finland, the town became a symbol of a stubborn resistance to what was seen as an inevitable trend (Säntti, 2010). The transformation in Seinäjoki can be seen not only in newspaper and magazine articles but also in the statistics. Of course, in comparison with the main cities in Finland the R&D figures are still low, but it is possible to argue that the town has taken several steps forward. Both R&D expenditure and R&D employment have increased, as has the level of highly educated people. More broadly, the region is no longer losing population and the regional centre, Seinäjoki, has been growing steadily.

As these quick examples show, many cities across the globe have faced increasing global competition and newly emerging economic dynamics (for Asian cases, see, for example, Cho and Hassink, 2009; Hatakenaka, 2004). The challenges and policy responses share many similarities but the place-based governance structures and social networks may lead to differences, not only in how successful the responses are, but also in the ways they are constructed in the first place. Indeed, some cities transform successfully while some continue in a downward spiral. As Parkinson *et al.* put it:

> [. . .] cities are different but share some common challenges. For example, all are attempting to increase or protect their economic competitiveness at national and sometimes European level. Many of them have been through processes of economic restructuring and are trying to find new economic functions and niches. They all face the challenge of balancing economic, social and environmental goals. All the cities wrestle with social and economic inequalities spread across different parts of their territory. They are all attempting to find ways of working in partnership with the private sector and to work successfully with national governments. All the places are attempting to develop territorial governance at scale so that decision-making arrangements work for the wider functional economic area or city-region – not just the narrow administrative city boundary. Their degree of success varies
>
> (Parkinson *et al.*, 2012: 39).

2.2 The key messages and basic questions

Studies and cases focusing on knowledge, learning and innovation, and related systems, have shown how territorial economies evolve on specific path dependencies, and how cities and regions may specialise their economies on technological innovations (lately also on non-technological innovations), and how smart diversification enables them to compete in the global economy, or how diversity and related variety are important for city development. Relatedly, innovation policy has gained more prominence in many parts of the world, and as institutions framing both economies and innovation differ between regions and countries, it is now a more or less established view in research, and in city development as well as innovation policy, that to make a difference, strategies need to be customised to suit the needs of the country, region, city and/or industry in question. At local and regional levels, economic and innovation policies draw more often than not on various theories and development models that highlight the importance of proximity, institutions, reciprocal knowledge exchange and interactive learning between firms and other relevant organisations (Halkier *et al.*, 2012). Recent theorising, as well as empirical evidence around knowledge bases (Asheim *et al.*, 2011) and combinatorial knowledge dynamics, additionally suggests that new types of territorial relations are emerging due to a qualitative shift from cumulative knowledge dynamics towards combinatorial knowledge dynamics (Grillitsch and Trippl, 2013). Cumulative knowledge dynamics refers to the degree to which new knowledge builds upon existing knowledge, while combinatorial knowledge dynamics builds upon the integration of separated knowledge (Strambach and Klement, 2012). The double challenge of any city is to construct conditions for local knowledge accumulation and combination, and simultaneously make sure that a city will not turn inwards but is connected to main knowledge hubs globally. As Cooke and Leyesdorf (2006: 6) boldly maintain, "the balance between knowledge and resources has shifted so far towards the former that knowledge has become by far the most important factor determining standards of living – more important than land, capital, or labour".

There now exists a large body of studies stressing that global sources of knowledge, and localised knowledge, are crucial in the competitiveness of city-regions. These knowledge pools may arise from the concentration of sectoral or cluster specific firms and other relevant organisations. Bathelt *et al.*, (2004) suggest that both "the information and communication ecology created by co-location of people and firms within the same industry and place or region and global pipelines, i.e. channels used in accessing knowledge external to city-region, offer advantages for organisations engaged in innovation and knowledge creation". As they state further, ". . . local buzz is beneficial to innovation processes because it generates opportunities for a variety of spontaneous and unanticipated situations, global pipelines are instead associated with the integration of multiple selection environments that open different potentialities and feed local interpretation and usage of knowledge hitherto residing elsewhere" (Bathelt *et al.*, 2004). The key observation, that the productivity and competitiveness of cities and regions are a function of knowledge generation, diffusion and valorisation, also serves as the point departure for this book. Scott simplifies all this by saying that the core of a city-region's competitiveness is its ability to construct global competitiveness on local competences (Scott, 1988).

Isaksen and Wiig Aslesen (2001) classify the theories of how cities position themselves as innovation and knowledge centres. They stress that cities are the first receivers of global knowledge, as they are often the first to seize innovations created in other countries, and these innovations are reworked and produced first in the largest cities. Cities are also breeding grounds for innovation. They stimulate innovation activity locally through localisation and urbanisation economies, and by the flow of tacit knowledge that requires proximity to be efficiently exchanged.

Cities are also the cores of national systems of innovation, as they host such assets as knowledge organisations, specialised firms, demanding customers, etc. They often hold important knowledge for more broadly feeding into innovation processes in the firms of a country (Isaksen and Wiig Aslesen, 2001). Following this line of thinking, a knowledge city may be defined as a place where the local milieu enables the intensive, continuous, diverse and complex creation and exploitation of new knowledge for the prosperity of a city (for more see, for example, Carrillo, 2006; Madanipour, 2011). The literature raises the following factors as important in the development and growth of knowledge cities, the many efforts to construct cities as main centres of innovation.

- **Quality higher education institutions** for education and to carry out scientifically high quality but also economically and socially relevant research to provide new knowledge and also solutions to old and new problems;
- **Leading private companies** that may act as patrons and funders of local universities and carry out research and development by themselves, and act as incubators of talent that will go on to create new companies and employment opportunities;
- **Small private companies** that diversify and broaden the economic base, offer employment opportunities, provide venture capital and other types of investments with opportunities;
- **Quality of life and place** that attracts and retains knowledge workers; and
- Local, regional, national and transnational **government commitment** to promote knowledge city development. Public policy can be an effective enabler but also allow continuity.

(Carrillo, 2006; Landry, 2006; Carrillo et al.,
2014; Florida, 2002)

A knowledge city is emergent in character. We can never know for certain what development strategies, services and products are important from the perspective of the future success of a city, nor can we know exactly what factors encourage companies and other important functions to put down their roots in a city. For these ends, cities need local buzz and global pipelines (Bathelt *et al.*, 2004), to simplify the contemporary policy recipe to its extreme. The main aim of many local economic development strategies is to cultivate specifically differentiated and locally rooted but extra-regionally connected knowledge pools, and to foster links between academia, industry and the public sector: to construct knowledge-based local advantages (see Asheim *et al.*, 2006). There also is a broad consensus that knowledge-based economic development is not somehow a spatially blind process but rather, is highly embedded in a particular socio-economic context (Tödtling *et al.*, 2013). Many city mothers and fathers, as well as other policy-makers, have subscribed to these ideas, and there is no lack of policy recommendations about how to boost transformation from industrial cognitions, structures and norms towards knowledge city development. The main focus here is not on knowledge city strategies as such, but on the kind of leadership that is needed to lead complex influence networks to these ends. As the main target of interest here is generative leadership, and the knowledge-based economic development of cities is the context for its study, there is no need to dig deeper into the knowledge-innovation-learning puzzle. This will be discussed alongside leadership, using specific cases to highlight how cities aim to transform themselves into something that is here crystallised in the concept of a knowledge city.

All that has been said in this chapter leads us back to the very basic questions about city development. As Storper (2013: 5) asks: why do some city-regions grow while the others decline? What differentiates city-regions that are able to sustain growth from those that are not? Why are some city-regions more productive and/or innovative than others? What is the relationship between material-physical structure and economic development, on the one hand, and institutional arrangements and economic development, on the other hand? And perhaps most interestingly, what are the principal regularities in urban and regional growth, and what are the events and processes that are not temporally or geographically regular but instead affect pathways of development processes (Storper 2013, 5)?

Storper's basic questions ought to be taken seriously, as, in spite of enthusiasm and many key insights, the learning, knowledge and innovation-oriented models have also run into several problems. First, they often conflate networks and cities (and regions), and unrealistically assume that intra-regional networks might be the principal instruments for local/regional learning and somehow automatically produce good results. Second, the fairly straightforward connection between the new models and a hunger for new policies and desired success stories have made the new concepts and models into mixtures of conceptual and policy elements which have created conceptual ambiguity (Rutten and Boekema, 2012; Rutten *et al.*, 2014). Policy concepts often run ahead of theory, not to mention empirical evidence, which would reach beyond case descriptions, while contrarian cases and more comprehensive and comparative enquiries challenging the mainstream theories are not common enough (Markussen, 1999). The promotion of knowledge-based economic development requires a well-established understanding of how city-regions generate development from within, and here the flexibility of existing institutions, governance structures and mind-sets emerges as crucial. Policy-makers have not traditionally been keen on flexibility, but it may be essential for stimulating innovation and creating a truly innovation-supporting local environment with strong global connections. The local environment needs to be transformed if a city wants to benefit from newly emerging knowledge, competencies and technologies, and contribute to their emergence.

At the same time we need to acknowledge that organisations and institutions do not usually adapt spontaneously, due to the many inertial forces, and thus generative leadership is central in achieving adaptation. All the cities used in the book as illustrative cases have aimed to adapt strategically, but more or less as a reaction to the crisis in hand; they have been forced to change, to adapt to a changing environment. Quite often the reactionary policies are based on seeds planted years or decades earlier, often in the form of people working in the future before the rest of us even realise that something is actually changing. In future crises, it should be asked more often than we do nowadays, what kind of functions and processes are essential in the unbroken procession of reinterpretation and reinvention, to enable entire city-regions to adapt strategically. In many city-regions that could be labelled resilient, and that have been capable of bouncing back from industrial decline, concerted actions to adapt to changing environments from within, strategically, have played a crucial role in economic development, and often in concert with various national policies.

The fact that policy-makers at many levels are so eager to grasp new emerging theories and development models may be a sign of hunger for success but also of certain kind of desperation to find new tools to construct development strategies in a situation that is characterised by a rapidly changing global economic landscape, on the one hand, and fiscal difficulties, on the other hand. We might end up asking, as suggested above, whether the economic development of cities is about deliberate efforts at all or if it is a purely emergent process. This would raise the question of the kind of leadership that is capable of navigating through the many and contingent intersections in which most cities are embedded (Collinge and Gibney, 2010a). Indeed, the world is full of emergent properties that are stronger than the abilities of city mothers and fathers. Relatedly, in many studies agency, performance and policy practice have not been paid adequate attention, and thus the tone is often overly structure and process-oriented, without a proper analysis of who does what, why and how (see, for example, Markussen, 1999; Sotarauta and Mustikkamäki, 2015). To conceptualise knowledge city development and generative leadership, this book follows, in its own way, such authors as Hassink (2102), Bathelt and Glücker (2003), Rutten and Boekema (2012) and Rutten *et al.* (2014) who adopt a relational perspective of the economic development of cities and regions, and adds temporal dimension to it in the end.

3 Governance and influence networks

3.1 Governance and leadership

The significance of governance structures for leadership in city development cannot be over-emphasised; in many ways they frame leadership processes and practices. As Beer states, the leadership of places cannot be examined in isolation, as the relationship between leaders and governmental or other powers either enables or constrains generative leadership significantly (Beer, 2014). Parkinson (1990: 21–22) argues that there are places where political differences lead to situations in which "no coherent response, negotiation or agreement among a broad range of political and social groups is possible". Fortunately, there also are places where coherent place leadership is a central part of a city's competitive advantage (Parkinson, 1990; Stimson *et al.*, 2009; Stough, 2003; Parkinson *et al.*, 2012). Interestingly, as leadership in cities and regions is gaining importance, the forms and modes of government have also been in flux, and in its own way, generative leadership responds to shifts from government to governance (Rhodes, 2000), from the generic trend of hierarchies to networks (Powell 1990), and the search for new approaches to managing complexity and "wicked issues" at the interstices of sector-based policy silos (Sotarauta, 1996; Klijn, 1996).

Importantly, it is seen that the distributed systems may be better suited to meet the emergent forces, and hence one of the key trends has been the forging of systems of national, regional and local governance in support of various organisations, to enable them to simultaneously compete, cooperate and create functioning networks for the economic development of cities. This, perhaps, has resulted in a gradual erosion of the traditional bases of political and economic power (Pierre, 2000). Alternatively, new modes of governance are emerging, as the traditional bases of political and economic power are not capable of matching the ever-more-networked economy. Although public policy-making has been taken closer to the new ideals of governance through devolved power, and by emphasising the self-guidance and cooperation, the procedures of the government continue to have their effect on structures, processes and attitudes. The rigid attitudes and structures of governments persist in many places and cause problems, as contemporary problems are the result of several inseparable factors, and their root causes cannot be traced back to individual factors (Liddle, 2010). In principle, the new forms of governance enable the adoption of more place-based approaches to economic development but, in practice, in many countries, the system is hovering somewhere between siloed government and collaborative governance, as explained by a Finnish leader from local government.

> The issue is that we should approach local and regional development from a holistic perspective, from a territorial thinking instead of sectorial. But, but ... these state agencies want to stick in their sectors and focus on their own field and keep others out. Many live and work in a tube, and thus integrative thinking is in paper but not in action.

In policy arenas that are of high-bounded rationality, it is difficult to know what might be the correct course of action to be shared among many instead of a few, and gaining an understanding of it is usually very demanding, and takes a great deal of time to achieve. Defining the problem, let alone designing appropriate solutions, is a difficult and daunting task (Stone, 1993; Stoker, 2000). As Hirst (2000, 259) points out, this kind of complexity and interdependence embedded in modern governance raises two crucial questions, first, "how to create an at least minimally effective division of labour in governance, one that will link together a complex set of very different bodies that, even in combination, cannot be considered to be a 'political community' ", and second "how to ensure at the different levels within this division of labour an effective presence of democratic voice – so that the actions of a body at one level do not systematically negate decisions at another" (Hirst 2000, 259). In the many efforts to solve these problems, the point of departure is not necessarily the search for right answers directly, as it is in the more traditional modes of government, but rather how people contending with issues from different sides and perspectives can join forces in the search for new questions and new answers. Governance depends on the interaction of several actors and on a selection of combined indirect and direct means that are not necessarily planned in advance by any single organisation. So, governance stresses that a number of agencies ought to be able to exchange resources and align their competencies if they are to promote economic development of cities effectively (Stone, 1993; Stoker, 2000). Governance aims to open new horizons for the coordination of social systems and, for the most part, the role of the public sector in that process. In a state-centric approach the main research problems are the extent to which the state has the political and institutional capacity to "steer", how the role of the state relates to the interests of other influential actors, and, in the way that governance acknowledges emergence better than earlier forms of government. Modern governance emerges from socio-economic-political processes on the basis of the interaction of relevant actors. Interactions in these networks are game-like, rooted in trust and regulated by the rules of the game negotiated and agreed by network participants (Rhodes, 2000).

Collinge and Gibney (2010b) divide governance into purposive and spontaneous, which brings us back to the question of the relationship between strategic intention and emergence. The ability for governance implies a tension between intention and emergence, and that this tension should be put to good use. According to Collinge and Gibney (2010b), purposive governance is an ordering process that is the direct expression of goals that are pursued consciously by human agents working alone or in concert. Spontaneous governance is an ordering process that is a function of self-organising mechanisms, which operate across human purposes without individual actors directly controlling this operation or its outcome as a whole. The economic forces constantly seeking new directions in cities are, most of the time, self-sustaining, without any need for special attention from public administration, and thereby modern governance stresses supporting the emergent models instead of aiming to control them directly. Leadership through increasing interdependence and plurality presupposes the ability to act as part of both purposive and spontaneous governance processes in the midst of a pluralistic and overlapping field of actors, which is no more private than public, and in which the borders between teams playing knowledge city game are fine indeed. Kickert (1993) states that it is essential to see that the leader of a complex governance system is not some external third party, an actor bringing to bear influence from above and outside, but the effect of different actors on each other and on themselves.

The key question here concerns whether existing or new forms of urban governance can release the learning and innovation potential of a city, and thus also reduce the tensions of co-existence and power sharing in multiple webs of relations (Healey *et al.*, 1995; Bryson and Crosby, 1992). As there are many games going on at the same time, and as it is often fairly difficult to *a priori* identify the truly important games, it is also hard to know how to play the development game when it arises on the agenda. It follows that urban governance is a concept that highlights the general nature of the structures and processes that connect public sector activities to each other and to various other actors and communities. In governance, the attention is focused on interaction, and therefore "urban" is understood here, drawing on the arguments of Healey *et al.* (1995), as an ensemble of diverse social relations, with different referents and spatial dimensions, which co-exist in the confined arena of urban areas. The particular nature of the ensemble of relations to be found in a place makes a difference to the possibilities for economic development. Healey *et al.* (1999) state that they are "concerned with how local governance could get to play a role in reducing the vulnerability of local economies, societies and environments to damaging external pressures while at the same time promoting local economic health and quality of life". Generative leadership, ideally, is the force providing governance processes with direction, and the social glue keeping them together.

Governance also recognises and acknowledges that many activities have shifted from formal organising to more informal networking; therefore, network negotiation and coordination can be confounded by the political context in which they are embedded, and new modes of governance thus also push leaders to find novel means of influence not only within the boundaries of the organisations and communities that authorise them, but across many boundaries in order to reach organisations and communities where their actions and words may have influence, although they have no formal authorisation (Sotarauta, 2005). In cities, leadership

Table 3.1 Difference in the formulation of policy processes in government and governance thinking (modified from Sotarauta 1996 and 1999)

	Government	Governance
System	Bureaucratic, centrally coordinated and sectored, emphasis on tradition of doing things alone	Devolved, emphasis on doing together and networking, also mutual dependence recognised and accepted
Problems	Tame, can be relatively precisely defined	Increasingly wicked, hard to define
Objects	Clear, basic assumption of shared nature of society's main goals and lack of conflict	Differentiated and ambiguous; may also be contradictory
Resources	Resources believed to grow continuously, political attention on allocation of resources; existing constructs and actions not questioned	Needs constantly exceed resources, ample economic operating environment formed from organisations capable of negotiation and ready to seek and start-up joint projects
Organisation of co-operation	Institution-based policy arena	Issue-based policy arena

Source: modified from Sotarauta, 1996 and 1999

is often seen in terms of formally constituted hierarchical power, but the shift towards governance has profound implications for the exercise of leadership. In the new mode of governance, new partners are constantly sought, coalitions formed and dissolved at all levels of action, and thus such questions as what is to be done, and how, are constantly negotiated and communicated in various forums. Hambleton (2003) phrases it as follows: "Out goes the old hierarchical model of the city "boss" determining policy for city council services and imposing it on the bureaucracy, and in comes the facilitative leader reaching out to other stakeholders in efforts to influence decisions in other agencies that affect the local quality of life". Of course, there are many old bureaucratic city bosses around, and it may well be that facilitative leaders are a minority in many places. We can only assume here that their share is increasing. Table 3.1 summarises the main differences of government and governance in the discussion of generative leadership that is set against governance thinking.

3.2 The space local leaders have

It is possible to understand leadership as a generative force in a governance system and related policy networks. We therefore need to adopt a systemic view on generative leadership that sees beyond the traits and behaviours of an individual and recognises the limits to instrumentally steer societal development. As Parkinson *et al.* (2012) conclude, leadership is a systemic quality and not individual. It culminates in influencing economic development activity across many social fields and administrative, sectorial, territorial, and institutional borders (Normann, 2013). In their empirical analysis of European second-tier cities, Parkinson *et al.* (2012) show how European cities face challenges that are created by administrative fragmentation, limited local autonomy and financial pressures at all levels. This often leads to competition and conflict between government authorities that again results in slow and cumbersome decision-making, little integrated land, transportation and economic planning. Interestingly, Parkinson *et al.* (2012) observe that these challenges are most acute in the most successful, rapidly growing second tier cities. Many cities struggle to align territory, governance and economy, and to find effective ways of dealing with growth. According to their analysis, strategic decision-making at city regional level is crucial to economic performance but also difficult to achieve. Fortunately, there are examples of cities that have managed to integrate different policies to promote development, and utilise national and transnational programmes by blending them with local initiatives and resources (Parkinson *et al.*, 2012). In addition to other factors, leadership has a role to play in achieving this style of governance.

Leadership in a governance setting needs to be seen as being both horizontal and vertical, and when flavoured with the concept of multi-level governance (the participation of different levels of government), as relationships between the participants at and across various levels. It is important to understand the balance of powers between central and local government and the broad policy context in which the city operates in its local economic development efforts. Several studies show that countries with a strong tradition of centralised government are, as Beer and Clower (2014) point out, less likely to foster the rise of place-based leaders and are more likely to follow models of government that impede regional or local initiatives. Centralised systems of government have a tendency to focus narrowly on specified outputs and outcomes, while devolved systems are more likely to adopt a more strategic but also place-specific and nuanced approach to city development (Stimson *et al.*, 2009). In contrast to centralised views of governance, Hildreth (2011) introduces three models of localism that help us to understand the space local leaders may, or may not, have. (a) *Conditional localism* highlights the role of central government in improving service delivery and local economic development policy, and in ensuring policy coherence from the top down. It acknowledges local autonomy but under strong central supervision (Hildreth, 2011); (b) In *representative localism* local actors and governance have a clear constitutional position in a democratic system, and (c) *community localism* is built on the devolution of power to local community groups and third sector actors and their direct involvement in governance structures and the execution of policies (Hildreth, 2011; see also Bentley *et al.*, forthcoming).

Local leaders are usually provided with more space and resources in such governance systems where elected mayors and local councils are provided with space to act strategically. In localised systems, local leaders are perceived to offer not only mobilisation and directions for development efforts but also scope for transparency, advocacy and strategic capacity (Bentley *et al.*, forthcoming).

This is not usually the case in centralised systems. Stimson *et al.* (2009) characterise the way systems of government enable or constrain the emergence of local leadership. Importantly, they argue that some of the more devolved systems of government (e.g. the US and Germany) are highly favourable to the emergence of local leaders, while centralised systems of government (Australia, the UK) generate adverse conditions for local leaders. As the House of Commons Communities and Local Government Committee (2011: 7, cited in Meegan, 2012) puts it:

> England is one of the developed world's most centralised democracies. The centre controls virtually all taxation, and power has followed money. Over the period since 1945 power and authority have moved upwards within the English political system, as expectations of government responsibilities for improving individual lives have risen with the advent of the welfare state, and as parliamentary and governmental attention has turned from governing overseas territories to directing domestic policy.

Marshall *et al.* (2006) maintain that, as power is highly centralised in the UK, city leaders have their hands tied with respect to economic development, largely because councils remain fiscally highly dependent on the national government. This again leads to a limited ability to direct expenditure to where it is most needed locally. For example, the powers held by Leeds as a city are relatively limited, and like other cities in England, it finds itself on the receiving end of an often rapidly changing array of policies from central government departments and national agencies that need to be joined together at local level (Evans, 2013; Meegan, 2012). There are other European cases that reveal how the centralisation of power is worsened by the lack of strong, democratically elected local and/or regional government and fragmented metropolitan governance (e.g. Timisoara, Romania), while some other cases reveal that cities in decentralised states (e.g. Katowice, Poland) may in practice face the same kinds of issues as those in centralised unitary states (e.g. Cork, Ireland), as decentralisation of responsibilities may not have been matched by the decentralisation of financial resources (Parkinson *et al.*, 2012).

In contrast to England, the Finnish local government has a bit more space to manoeuvre as it enjoys strong, constitutionally-guaranteed, local autonomy and the strength of local government is enabled by its fiscal powers: municipalities have a right to levy taxes (local income tax; real estate tax; a share of corporate tax) and collect fees and charges. On the average, in 2013 tax revenue represented 47% and sales of good and services 27% of the total revenue of the Finnish local government, while central government transfers represented only 19% (Local and Regional, 2015). In Finland, more broadly, cities and regions are seen as the authors of their own development, instead of mere recipients and objects of top-down policies (Vartiainen, 1998). Under the Regional Development Act, local government and the state share responsibility for regional development. In practice, the Finnish governance system for local and regional development is a complex constellation of local, sub-regional, regional and central government agencies, which is partly embedded in the regional policy of the European Union. The Ministry of Employment and Economy is responsible for local and regional development at national level, while at the local level, municipalities use their own resources to promote local development. In the 1990s, sub-regional cooperation between municipalities was institutionalised and several local solutions to regional co-operation were created, with experiences varying greatly across the country. Overall, the institutional arrangements for local and regional development in Finland are relatively complex and publicly led, with a set of development agencies operating at different levels. For these reasons, Finnish local and regional development practices are largely indirect in nature, and the success of development strategies is dependent of the functionality of both formal and informal policy networks.

The constraints put in place by governance systems should not, however, be over-estimated in any study of generative leadership, as the best of the generative leaders are leaders because they can stretch the constraints they face and navigate through sometimes complex events, networks and governance systems. They not only initiate new processes but also change the rules of the game. Therefore, it is not suggested here that there would not be a need for local generative leadership in centralised systems, or that there might not be such actors who would take the lead – it is simply suggested that their space and resources to manoeuvre are different from those found in devolved systems, and usually less. Importantly, Hu and Hassink (forthcoming) show that there is indeed a need for more comparative studies in order to say anything definitive about the space generative leaders take in centralised systems. As they argue, even in authoritarian China, local leaders have space to influence, and municipal political leaders have institutional power to influence local state subordinates, which to some extent can help leaders to integrate more broadly into local contexts. Simultaneously, the transitional context of China means the central government encourages local proactive economic reforms that again provide leeway for local leaders to play outside the existent institutional box to implement "local experimentations", while without the pressures of local critical voices (e.g. non-governmental civic groups) (Hu and Hassink, forthcoming). Hu and Hassink further argue that the taken-for-granted dichotomy of "effective place leadership in democratic countries" and "less-effective place leadership in non-democratic counties" needs to be further clarified through more empirical studies in non-democratic contexts.

At all events, the roles provided by governance systems are important, as they dictate what kind of resources, and what kind of formal position is given to local development work, and thus also to leaders. The financial capacity of cities and regions greatly affects the local capacity to manoeuvre and the space local leaders have for their action. Especially important is the extent to which they rely upon national grants, transfers and financial equalisation or can raise their own revenue (Bentley *et al.*, forthcoming). What follows is the observation that the focus in local governance should not lie solely on the fiscal health of local governments, or their capacity to deliver centrally dictated services (Katz and Bradley, 2013).

This again signifies that the key issue in achieving good governance is the extent to which responsibilities are shared and roles are transparent and well articulated, and therefore the question is also whether leadership is shared or not (Karlsen and Larrea, 2012). All this is supported by case studies across Europe that remind us that the question is essentially about collective strategic decision-making capacity and the functionality of the governance system as a whole, and to lesser extent simply about the division of powers and resources (Parkinson *et al.*, 2012). To put it simply: a well-functioning governance system enables local leaders to focus on what needs to be done and thus empowers them, while a less well-functioning governance system may lead to internal fighting and thus limit the capacity of local leaders to act for the city instead of the governance system itself.

Barcelona, for example, has been shown to demonstrate significant strategic decision-making capacity. The city's innovative mix of cultural activity and urban regeneration has been emphasised by a unique governance style based upon strong citizen support (Gonzalez and Healey, 2005), which few have dared to challenge (Degen and Garcia, 2012). Its leaders, both public and private, have responded to the massive challenges the city has faced and skilfully exploited existing resources and emerging opportunities to the city's advantage. Interestingly, Barcelona operates in a decentralised governance system that is a "complex multi-level territorial governance system", in which regional government is more powerful and important than either national or local government (Parkinson *et al.*, 2012). Parkinson *et al.* (2012) highlight also the functionality of the German territorial governance system, which supports vertical integration and the sharing of key functions among several public authorities. The federal government funds urban and regional partnership experiments and major schemes are the subjects of extensive negotiations between federal, state and city governments. It is a political and administrative system that requires the different levels to work together.

A comparative empirical study on place leadership in Finland and Australia reveals how governance structures influence the ways place leadership emerges and is shaped and constructed (Sotarauta and Beer, forthcoming). For example, in both countries, local governments are considered an important source of place leadership, but the leadership role of local governments is recognised more strongly in Finland than in Australia, and its modes of operation are different from Australia, as the institutional position of local government is significantly stronger there. While there are many similarities in manifestations of place leadership in both countries, it is also obvious that both the compositions of networks and expressions of place leadership differ along the governance structures. Place leadership in Finland is embedded in the well-developed public sector institutions, with specialist staff and specialist training. In Australia, place leadership depends more on the voluntary efforts of individuals from the private sector and various communities. Its relationship with government is indirect, characterised by a tension between the centralising tendency of central governments and the need for independently-minded local leaders to engage with governments to secure resources. Beer (2014) shows how in Australia place leadership is often subversive of the agendas of central governments. He argues that local leaders aim to reposition themselves and their region through contestation and more subtle resistance instead of working in collaboration with the central government, as often is the case in Finland (Sotarauta and Beer, forthcoming). In regional Australia, contestation may be the only way that local actors can influence policy outcomes, and the persistence of local generative leaders may overcome the apparently powerful but short-lived interests of the centralised state (Beer, 2014). So, Australian place leadership is less open than in Finland, and this is reflected in a reluctance to debate regional needs publicly, as well as a lower level of engagement with various stakeholders (Sotarauta and Beer, forthcoming). In practice, no system is pure in its functions, as is shown by two different leaders from a Finnish region describing the same governance system.

> It is a beautiful system, in principle, localities can decide on their own matters, but I think that the State sees us as so dumb that we can't make any wise decisions and thus the reality is different. What can you do, if you do not have real authority, independent decision-making powers on issues that truly matters.

> There are a lot of investments in expertise and education here. It's been a clear strategy involving local government, regional development authorities and the State authorities. Great collaboration, that's what it is.

Sotarauta and Beer conclude that leadership in Finland is institutionally based, and in Australia it is individualised. Their findings reveal how national governance arrangements shape and frame place leadership. Finland is a coordinated market economy, and place leadership is one manifestation of the many efforts to enhance strategic interaction among firms, public agencies and other actors. This type of interaction is common in coordinated market economies. In a liberal market economy such as Australia, place leadership operates in more a competitive environment, where non-market relationships are valued less highly. The observations of Sotarauta and Beer (forthcoming) support Hidle and Normann (2011) who say that leadership cannot be fully explained only in terms of levels of trust, social capital and institutional set-up. Importantly, they claim that issues related to how power is institutionalised in governance systems need to be explored and explained in order to improve our understanding of processes associated with the construction of leadership.

In simplification, it can be argued that the generative leadership in governance arrangements may take following stylised but overlapping forms:

- **Collaborative and systemic** – involvement of many actors is embedded in the system. Local generative leadership emerges more from the formal governance system than outside it.
- **Confrontative and individualised** – development processes are based more on competition than collaboration. Local generative leadership emerges more from outside the formal governance system than inside it.

- **Authoritative** – governance and generative leadership based on formal centralised power and assigned leaders. Local generative leadership is strongly embedded in the formal governance system under central supervision.

When investigating generative leadership we need to recognise that leaders are not only embedded in the governance systems but also in the culture and various subcultures of a city, and also the cultures of the various economic sectors they work with and that are dominant in a city. John Gibney concluded his keynote speech in the Regional Studies Association's European Conference in 2011 by painting an interesting picture of place leadership. He said place leaders face many complex "wicked issues" in their contextually specific and ever-changing landscapes, which are continuously subject to unanticipated and episodic crises. All this is shaped by multiple identities of actors representing all possible walks of life with their own ways of knowing as well as rationales guiding their behaviour. For these reasons, local development efforts may be, and often are, emotionally charged – they may appear irrational to many. All this is in a governance system that is connected to other systems through multiple channels, and where nobody is in charge alone, but where leadership is the effect that actors have on each other. Generative leadership in cities, and all other forms of place leadership, is an intriguing subject of study, for exactly these reasons.

3.3 Influence networks and leadership

3.3.1 The anatomy of networks in a nutshell

This chapter explores the concept of the influence network, which seeks its inspiration from policy network literature, aiming to specify the concept of governance for the discussion of leadership. The role of networks has interested local and regional development community as well as investigators from other fields of enquiry for some time now. At first, academic debate revolved around the nature of political decision-making, the main axis of many debates being the division between pluralists and elitists (later corporatists). The debate centred on openness for participation by any organised group, as stressed by the pluralists, and such openness being a chimera as stressed by elitists and corporatists (Bruun, 2002). These debates lead increased emphasis on interests groups and the roles they play in public decision-making (Marsh, 1998; Klijn, 1996). The concept of policy network was adopted to enhance our understanding of the context in which actual policy processes take place (Klijn, 1996). Scharpf (1997), for example, argues that the focus of policy science before "network turn" had been too much on interactions between particular organisations, instead of the longer-term relations between policy-making organisations. So, as indicated above, policy networks belong to the new forms of governance that complement top-down policy-making as well as market-oriented attempts to make government more dynamic (Klijn, 1996). In general, networks have won ground partly as a result of the failures of the previous siloed government models, and partly as a result of the increasing complexity of modern policy problems (Kickert *et al.*, 1997).

The concept of the influence network is used here instead of a policy network (Kenis and Schneider, 1991), as in generative leadership the question is more about influencing other actors for city development than the formation and implementation of a specific policy. An influence network is a form of policy network model with special focus on the generation of conditions that allow something new to emerge. A key means for generative leaders to tackle the challenge of dynamic transition and thus boost the emergence of conditions for collective action was once to form a growth coalition that often served fairly narrowly defined intentions and interests (Molotch, 1976; Logan and Molotch, 1987). Stoker (2000: 94) illustrates the change in thinking by saying: "The initial governance focus was on coalition formulation as the mechanism for achieving coordination. Yet this narrow focus needs to be expanded to consider wider coordination mechanisms both in recognition of what is happening in city politics and in order to gain a wider understanding that might in turn aid policy-makers, practitioners, and urban citizens."

When the concept of influence network is applied to the promotion of knowledge city development it is used to identify and analyse the entity of actors involved in the development activities. Influence network refers to those key actors who, through their own actions and mutual cooperation, have an effect on the knowledge city development. Following Kickert *et al.* (1997: 6), influence networks are defined as "more or less stable patterns of social relations between interdependent actors, which take shape around common targets of interest and observed development needs". The notion of interdependence is crucial here. While much of the policy network as well as regional innovation system and policy literature are traditionally oriented more towards structures of these interdependencies than human agency and processes, this book aims to do the contrary, and argues that any successful effort to boost knowledge-based development of a city is not only dependent on resources, competencies and powers of more than one actor but also generative leaders that make it all move forward. These interdependencies are understood well at a strategic level but at a more pragmatic level, where action is called for, it may be revealed that the true nature of interdependencies was not grasped after all, and this is one of the reasons why generative leadership appears as important.

Influence networks are not static and hierarchically determined constellations, but dynamic living organisms that change as they go. In influence networks, individual actors exist not by themselves, but always in relation to each other, and as such, they are not only characterised by multiple objectives but also by multiple values and identities, and thus networks may also be emotionally charged. The kind of interaction exhibited by influence networks not only reflects complexity but also is in itself complex, dynamic and pluralistic. Generative leaders are not trying to avoid this kind of complexity and uncertainty but to take advantage of it. This differs from operational models constructed by the hierarchical procedures and competitive mechanisms of the market (Normann, 2013). One important advantage of the influence network concept is that it helps us to understand not only formal institutional arrangements but also highly complex informal relationships. There is considerable variation between cities as to the tightness and density of these networks but what is obvious is that the move towards networked mode of action is also reflected in innovation policy, for example, which for a long time was understood only as an outcome of rational decision-making and something for which only the public sector was responsible (Witt, 2003), but that is nowadays seen more as a multi-actor process in which policy content is affected by all stages and levels of policy-making and thus many networks (Kuhlmann, 2001; Sotarauta and Kosonen, 2013).

Ideally, influence networks do not rest on hierarchical relations but on ties characterised by loyalty, solidarity, trust and reciprocal support (Stoker, 1997). This suggests that influence networks are self-organising entities, but the labelling of networks as self-organising is usually fairly carelessly done. It is proposed here that it would be naïve to argue that networks can somehow be hierarchy- and power struggle-free territories (see Flyvbjerg, 1998). It may simply be that in networks hierarchies are shaped differently to what we were used to in government structures, and generative leadership may provide us with one of the lenses required to look more deeply in the relationship between networks and power. In networks, hierarchies are not based on positions only but largely on visions, skills, interaction, influence and perhaps also charisma. This suggests that not all agents involved in networks are equal. While generative leadership in network settings is distributed, so are responsibilities; roles are not equal or interchangeable, and there is much to be learnt about how power and hierarchies are manifested in network settings.

What follows is that knowledge city development takes the form of "organic" organisation that is decentralised and project-based, with strong horizontal as well as vertical communication and coordination, and which crosses many institutional and functional borders and barriers even though it is deeply embedded in a given system of governance. Ideally, the role of the public sector is to empower other actors, acting as a network partner instead of grand leader. Of course, the networked promotion of knowledge cities does not exist in its pure form, it is tangled in many ways with other forms of organisation, bureaucracy and markets. It is an approach that allows us to grasp the continuously unfolding development efforts by reaching beyond the formal and visible, the spectacle of authority. Influence networks accept and draw their motivation from the emergence of increasing global interdependencies and the acceptance of mutual dependence between all those who would like to see their city find novel avenues of development. The concept of the influence network narrows down the scrutiny of the otherwise almost endless scope of potential actors who have influence on city development. It also helps us to direct our attention to generative leaders instead of government structures.

As will be shown in Chapter 6, generative leadership is largely about influencing the independent decisions and actions of autonomous actors, but also about being the target of other actors' efforts to influence. This is one of the key reasons why various network approaches have emerged as central in our efforts to understand not only the global knowledge economy, but also efforts to construct local knowledge-based advantages. In influence networks, generative leaders need to master the norms, regulations and thinking patterns of several fields – like master decathletes they need to be able to move beyond their own specialities to take leadership positions. Two Finnish development officers, working for two different city governments, explain the importance and challenges of influence networks as follows. The first quote highlights the organic nature of influence networks and the second that they are not independent of existing power structures.

> If our network is good, smooth, versatile, agile and all that . . . it is much better for our efforts than a permanent agency of some kind. Network enables us flexibly to integrate special expertise into the development work and exploit it.

> [. . .] it is all about networks, I need to shepherd networks and make people talk and understand what this [city development] is all about, I need to convince them. But, my mandate is limited, officially I mean, it's all about mandates, and power, can I, should I try to influence what the big cheeses do, I know I should, but [. . .]

Generative leadership can emerge from the decisions and actions of many organisations but it can also be a product of the actions of individuals working collaboratively across the organisational boundaries (Collinge and Gibney, 2010a; Kroehn *et al.*, 2010). It is clear that generative leadership does not need to originate from one or even the same social sphere or sector in different places and governance systems. Bennett *et al.* (2003) argue that leadership in networks is distributed, and as such it is open to whoever should take or be considered to be in a leadership role in a particular setting. As such, leadership is "open in terms of including more than the conventional net of leaders and does not set any particular limit to how large is the leadership category" (Bennett *et al.*, 2003). For example, leadership may be attributed to individuals who are leading other individuals, organisations, inter-organisational networks in the place, or the entire place. It may also be attributed to the organisations leading individuals, other organisations, networks or clusters, and perhaps even to inter-organisational networks or clusters leading individuals and organisations (applying Huxham and Vangen, 2000). In all the latter cases, of course, human agents act on behalf of systems to "make things happen" through the actions of others. The list of potential partners in an influence network, and also sources of leadership is a long one:

- *R&D institutions*: university or faculty leadership; renowned professors; research institutions; knowledge parks; technology transfer institutions; consultancies; larger R&D projects;
- *Industry*: interest organisations; cluster project organisations; larger firms with regional anchorage; local entrepreneurs;
- *Public administration*: policy instrument and support infrastructure; leading bureaucrats both at national and regional/city level; publicly owned firms. Both private (venture capital) and public funding bodies; banks typically with a mandate to develop the region/firms in the region; regional research funds;

- *Influential individuals*: wealthy philanthropists; entrepreneurs; business owners; charismatic-, cultural-, intellectual-, sports personalities; previously elected representatives/political leaders.
- *Media*: local and national media organisations; and
- *Elected representatives*: political leaders, city mayors, leaders of local and regional development organisations, national level representatives, etc.

(Norman, 2013: 33; see also Sotarauta and Beer, forthcoming)

At all events, the importance of influence networks is supported by empirical evidence from several case studies. Drawing on Bruun's study of the bio-grouping-focused local economic policy process in Turku (Finland), we can argue that a policy process is a combination of new and old ways of acting and deciding, as well as of new and old coalitions; a complex, constantly evolving influence network.

> One of the striking features of the BioTurku trajectory is that it did not follow established decision-making channels, but was rather created through a mixture of old and novel forms for decision-making. Thus, horizontal collaboration between people and organisations (sometimes formalised, sometimes informal) was at least equally important as the vertical decision-making hierarchies of, for instance, the city and the universities. Seen from a BioTurku-perspective, the locus of initiative has been on constant move, and the bio-grouping has been dynamic, self-transforming, rather than a static structure.
>
> (Bruun, 2002: 81)

Bruun's observations tell us the story of a simultaneous search for new policy content and for new ways and combinations to achieve these aspirations. Similarly, Normann (2013) describes the development efforts in Agder, Norway by saying "[. . .] these strategies were planned and implemented as a result of network processes. The leadership behind these processes was not rooted in one political party, neither was there a single person or institution behind it. It was rather a collection of people from different institutions who worked together based on a shared vision of how the region should develop." Whatever the focus in the case under scrutiny – well-being, information and communication technology, biotechnology or creative industries, to name the few of fairly common elements – an influence network is never a single solid entity but a constantly evolving web of social relationships that is organised around both shared and differing expectations and objectives. They vary from loosely organised, irregularly interacting networks to focused and managed collaborative patterns.

3.3.2 Three types of influence networks

Through a generative leader lens, influence networks may be grouped into three generic types: strategic influence network, focused influence network and web of potentiality.

In principle, **strategic influence networks** involve all actors having a stake in the economic development of a city. In practice, compositions of strategic influence networks vary greatly between cities, if they exist at all, and they also vary in time. They are strategic as they pool actors with a goal of influencing the economic development of a city in the long term. They are often loosely organised, as only some of the actors belonging to them have been assigned the task of promoting knowledge city development, and therefore, many of the actors participate in network activities via their own interests and temporal restrictions, simultaneously having an indirect effect on the development of a city. In spite of the shared interest of participating actors in boosting knowledge city development, the strategic influence network is rendered loose by the fact that it may not necessarily have an established organisational form or permanent forums created for its purposes (even though in some cases it may have). Moreover, the strategic influence networks are generally organised in different combinations around different issues. They have their conversations in many different forums ranging from media to local strategic planning processes to conferences and seminars to meetings to projects to informal conversations, and thus, they are not only characterised by multiple objectives, and both weak and strong ties but also by multiple identities and ways of operation. By identifying the members of a strategic influence network, and who leads them towards more focused networks, we might learn much about how a social community organises itself to frame, analyse and discuss the main challenges and issues of a city – how a city is in search of new collective development strategies and/or aims to change existing ones.

Generative leaders often aim to launch **focused influence networks** that rely on strong ties and well-defined operational models. They usually have well specified objectives, and they also are project-based and thus temporally limited. In many cases, strategic influence networks are breeding grounds for more focused networks, and conversely, focused influence networks feed strategic influence networks with strategic issues, opportunities, threats and concrete development needs. The third network type involves all those potential partners who are not involved in development efforts but who might be interested in contributing to collective efforts, who might benefit from participating or who would like to participate to defend their own self-interest. It is labelled here as the **web of potentiality**.

> It is not possible to involve everybody, it'd be a horrendous effort to make everybody to understand the main issues, or think similarly. We need to find something we all can share, something that is good for you and me, and that way find a way for this network to work collaboratively. The networks should be open, in spite all of this, this kind of selective activation I mean, and our network should be inclusive and not exclusive. If you have something to offer, you can join it.

(A leader from a regional council)

The three spheres of influence networks are summarised as follows (Linnamaa and Sotarauta, 2000):

- **Web of potentiality** – all those actors who may have a stake in the development efforts but do not contribute to them or are not involved in networks. The web of potentiality reminds us that influence networks are not stable but organic, and generative leaders are always in search of new partners who might be connected to a strategic and/or focused influence networks.
- **Strategic influence network** – loosely organised, not centrally managed, with a constantly evolving composition to search for strategic directions and generation of strategic awareness.
- **Focused influence network** – formally organised, with a coordinator or a manager assigned, and with clear objectives and a well-specified composition to tackle identified and defined development need:
    - *Search network* focuses on a selected theme to benchmark other cities or learn from the field internationally or nationally. The main purpose is to search for and frame new strategies and/or development projects.
    - *Support network* is a personal level network that is constructed or that emerges spontaneously to support individual generative leaders in their own work, enables sharing of experiences and learning from colleagues.
    - *Prevention network* emerges or is constructed to prevent a common and identifiable threat from damaging a city one way or another.
    - *Exploitation network* emerges or is constructed to exploit an identifiable opportunity.
    - *Attraction network* emerges or is constructed to attract some important resources to a city; private and public investments, specialised labour, conferences, etc.
    - *Investment network* emerges or is constructed to pool funding for a major investment.

All these types of influence networks are simplified illustrations to paint a picture not only of highly dispersed and continuously evolving social relations, but also of the focus of their development efforts. The influence network classification does not suggest that public policies or development strategies and programmes would not play a role in the many efforts to enhance knowledge city development, on the contrary; but here they are simply seen as the products of networks, resources to be exploited locally and forums where network members may collectively contemplate development issues. All the networks briefly described above are important in the daily work of generative leaders. It is worth noting, however, that the rules, norms and codes of behaviour tend to differ from each other in different kinds of governance systems networks. Our Finnish interviewees constantly stressed the importance of combining informal and loosely organised modes of action with focused development efforts and formal governance systems – and vice versa. Three Finnish local leaders, greatly involved in development efforts in their own cities, but also at a national level, illustrate the relationship between formal and informal development efforts, or worlds, as follows.

It [local economic development] is a continuous process of communication, what's up in your organisation, and what they are planning over there, what issues are emerging, and things like that . . . and then we have the formal side of the coin. We have several official groups in which we discuss all this through. We have politicians; it is important to discuss what they want, what their will is. And the officially binding decisions are made, official strategies . . . But, but, if we had only these official meetings, nothing would happen, they don't create co-operation, or proper philosophical discussions about what this is all about. People can't even see this kind of hidden work but without it no official decisions would be made.

[. . .] there is a formal and informal world. The informal world is much more influential and effective, I mean that people know each other, they are in contact with each other all the time, and talk, talk a lot, and thus I know what the others see as important, what's boiling in their organisations, what might go through the political decision-making, stuff like that. And then we have all these official groups, where we prioritise the development projects officially. Because of the informal world, we know what's possible and what's not, where the potential fight is, and such.

It is important to have a hunch about what the political will is, or wills are, it's not always the same as officially proclaimed. What I am trying to say is that in the informal world, there is a lot of background work and nobody gets credit, that is forgotten when the decisions are made, but that is time consuming, truly. But it is the soil where the political and business decisions grow . . . Yeah, without personal networks, I would be a dead soul, useless.

Even when discussing leadership in knowledge city development with regard to influence networks, we should be careful not to over-emphasise them. It is possible to scrutinise the new forms of governance using the concept of network as a focusing device, but at the same time it is worth reminding, again, that the traditional government silos exist and do well in many countries, and that they form the formal playground for many generative leaders too. In a study focusing on Finnish policy networks and leadership (Sotarauta *et al.*, 2007), most of the interviewees divided their personal working environment into four independent but overlapping categories: (a) one's own organisation, (b) the governance system, (c) formal policy networks, and (d) informal influence networks. The organisation that pays the salary, and to which one is accountable, is of course important to any local leader and a self-evidently determinant of how people behave and aim to influence the course of events. Both the governance system as a whole and the home organisation shape actors' understandings of what is feasible and acceptable and what is not, and thus they influence expectations and provide incentives for individual generative leaders. The national and European development systems were seen as an institutional framework that both enable and constrain their development efforts. Interestingly, if interviewees saw an organisation as a home base and the system as one of the main playing fields and a source of resources, they saw networks as channels for new ideas, information, resources, insights, and effective implementation. Simplifying from the hundreds of interviews carried out in Finland, we might argue that from the point of view of an individual generative leader, the promotion of (knowledge) city development is an endless stream of more or less interconnected processes and networks that often are fairly indistinct, and are difficult to read and make sense of. One of the key challenges is to master all this. One way to master it is to know the system well but aim to influence it through people. Again, in the words of Finnish generative leaders:

> The system here, in Finland, is very dispersed. It is proactive but fragmented . . . you have to find those individuals who are the nodes of networks, or should I say, resources and influence flows. Information passes through them, they know more than others. I can't know everything or everybody, thus I need to find those who can help, and want to do it. I don't refer to an old boy, or an old sister, network of some kind, no. There may be those, but I just need to know who knows and who can execute things.

> In all these organisations [involved in local and regional development efforts] there are such persons who want to do more, who are willing to reach beyond their own work and to discuss, develop, think how to change this region. They are willing to take the responsibility, to be involved. . . . So, it is not possible to say that certain kinds of organisations are more important than the others [in official promotion of regional development] but that certain people are the key.

The challenge to mobilise, coordinate and direct these kinds of influence networks is formidable. The classic, mostly intra-organisational inspired, leadership and management perspectives so dominant for more than a century in public administration and in the corporate world are, according to Agranoff and McGuire (2001), simply not applicable to multi-organisational, multi-governmental, multi-sectoral and thus multi-vision, multi-strategy and multi-value forms of governing and promoting local development. Leadership in networks is not a trivial issue for city leaders; it is among the most demanding sets of everyday challenges for many of them. Earlier studies of policy networks and network leadership show that place leaders (Harmaakorpi and Niukkanen, 2007), as well as other development champions, are relatively incapable of expressing themselves clearly about how networks ought to be managed and led. They have a hard time positioning themselves in a networked world where many of the stable structures are in flux.

What is interesting is that, in influence networks, there is very little spontaneous use of the term "leadership" (Linnamaa and Sotarauta, 2000; Linnamaa, 2004; Sotarauta *et al.*, 2007). Actors who can be identified as acting like generative leaders, and who talk a lot about issues that are related to leadership, do not specifically use the word "leadership". Instead, they emphasise how network participants are equal, and how networks replace the "old word hierarchies, and leaders and all, stuff like that", as a Finnish leader emphasised in line with the governance and policy network literature. This observation corroborates the findings by Sydow *et al.* (2011: 1162), who say "one surprising outcome of the analysis is that, if not specifically prompted, discourse about leadership did not feature in network or cluster talk at all". There may be at least four reasons for this, according to Huxham and Vangen (2000: 1162): (a) leadership as a reflexive structuration is completely absent in these networks; (b) membership of these networks is of only marginal interest to an individual or an organisation; (c) leadership, although potentially identifiable in a network, is somewhat invisible; or (d) influence network members simply do not like to talk about leadership and, in particular, about being led. As Sydow *et al.* (2011) point out, this does not necessarily demonstrate a lack of leadership but rather its hidden nature, as behind structures. Indeed, several empirical studies demonstrate that **generative leadership is often hardly visible; it is a hidden form of leadership** shadowed by governance structures, networks and "network talk" that stresses equality (Sotarauta, 2009; 2010; Sotarauta and Mustikkamäki, 2015; Sydow *et al.*, 2011).

Based on Chapter 3, it can be concluded that generative leadership is shaped by the following circumstances:

- the governance structure of a country and the transnational influence it is exposed to;
- the nature and functionality of wider strategic influence networks in a city, and the character of relationships between its members;
- the focused networks of influence in a city, their composition, and the social and economic backgrounds of their members;
- the roles that leading persons are playing in the wider influence networks, and especially their relationship to national and international decision and policy-making; and,
- the resources and competencies that network members bring to a network.

While generative leaders often are oriented towards strategic issues, there are other actors involved in the influence networks; actors, who are more focused on managerial issues, criticism, enhancing collaboration or planning specific projects. In empirical studies focusing on generative leadership, there is a need to encompass also those actors who do not actively aim to lead the influence networks but who influence the networks as well as the many development efforts by supporting or opposing them (Battilana *et al.*, 2009). Therefore, it is important to acknowledge the many roles the opponents (actors who work to hinder or inhibit changes) may play in development processes. They do not merely express critical and opposing opinions but actually try to stop the developments they find undesirable. Also inhibiting or disrupting work aimed at preventing influence networks from accomplishing their goals is part of the game; it is the very nature of any development game. Table 3.2 summarises the six key roles identified by van de Ven and complemented by Sotarauta and Pulkkinen (2011). They are not elaborated further in this book, but they are introduced briefly here, as they may be used to specify the roles different actors play in influence networks.

Table 3.2 The six key roles in regional innovation journeys (van de Ven, 1999; see for
institutional entrepreneurship Sotarauta and Pulkkinen, 2011)

The role	Characteristics of the role
Institutional entrepreneur	Initiates divergent institutional changes and actively participates in the implementation of them.
Entrepreneur	Actively seeks for new opportunities and is willing to take financial and personal risk.
Sponsor	Advocates the change and is typically placed high in the organisation and/or system; supports the change process by loosening up institutional barriers and/or providing it with resources.
Mentor	Typically an experienced actor who coaches and advises other actors and especially institutional entrepreneurs and entrepreneurs throughout the process.
Critic	Plays the role of the devil's advocate by asking cunning questions that force the other actors to re-examine their assumptions and hold them against other criteria.
Institutional leader	The institutional leader is often not as directly involved in the change process as the other actors but has a position to assess the institutional change process from a more comprehensive angle than the other actors. Institutional leader often has a role of balancing the opposite roles of the sponsor/mentor and the critic.

Source: van de Ven, 1999; for institutional entrepreneurship, see Sotarauta and Pulkkinen, 2011

Next, we take a quick tour of three successful European cities to see how governance and leadership have come together in their development games. Three well-known experts on city development guide us, their sub-chapters are based on the extensive data collected in the Second Tier Cities in Europe Project (see Parkinson *et al.*, 2012).

3.4 Michael Parkinson: Barcelona – reinvention and repositioning through strategic leadership

Barcelona is a major second tier European city that has undergone massive economic transformation during the past three decades after the advent of democracy in Spain. It operates in a decentralised policy-making system with powerful regional government more important than either national or local government. It also operates in a complex multi–level territorial governance system. The capital of Catalonia, the largest economic region in Spain, Barcelona successfully reinvented itself following nearly 40 years of General Franco's dictatorship, strengthening its position in Europe and attracting foreign investment, international entrepreneurs and tourists. Although Barcelona is not immune to the global financial crisis and recession, it is an important example of urban economic transformation in a country that is Europe's fifth largest economy and the eleventh largest economy in the world.

In many ways it has outperformed the Spanish economy and in terms of Foreign Direct Investment and exports it is crucial to the future of the Spanish economy.

Barcelona's leaders in the public and private sector have responded to challenges and exploited opportunities to the city's advantage. Barcelona has significant strategic decision-making capacity. The city government has played a major role in the political economy of the region. That leadership has been high quality, often charismatic, and consistent. It has encouraged public private partnerships through its strategic planning processes but also through the myriad of economic development initiatives it has undertaken. Leaders used strategic planning and project-led development to successfully deliver an ambitious modernising and repositioning strategy over several decades. There are several reasons for Barcelona's success. First, it has shown consistent entrepreneurial and visionary leadership. Second, it has developed a model of public private partnership and citizen involvement which constantly evolves but whose essential principles remain the same. Third, it has made strategic planning not an add-on but a standard way of doing business in the city. Fourth, it has focused upon quality, which increasingly differentiates cities from each other. Fifth, it has internationalised its ambitions and its reach. Sixth, it has systematically worked on the fundamentals of the economy as well as some of the more dynamic sectors of the economy like tourism, biomedics, culture, and ICT. The seventh secret is its constant self-assessment and willingness to compare its performance with the best places within Europe and globally. The city has never rested on its laurels but is always willing to learn from competitors about how to improve. Finally, Barcelona's leaders have understood that although city government matters, city governance matters even more. The city council has recognised that being well run and efficient is important – especially in a period of scarce resources. But Barcelona's leaders have understood something bigger about city government. Providing well run local services are a necessary but not a sufficient condition of success for a city. They have recognised that the city council should not be a provider of services alone. It has to be a leader and a shaper of place. The idea of place shaping is now very fashionable. But Barcelona virtually invented the idea. It has demonstrated leadership in creating the kind of place that people globally and locally want to live, work and invest in. That is the key to its success.

Barcelona has significantly improved its performance on all drivers of economic competitiveness in recent years. It has a large traditional manufacturing economy which is dominated by small firms but is also encouraging innovation through its universities and in key sectors of the economy like biomedicine, logistics, and design. The Barcelona economy is a mixed one with strengths in traditional as well as modern sectors. It does not have all its eggs in one basket. The city has made significant efforts to improve its skill base. It has also significantly upgraded its connectivity in recent years. Its airport, rail, port and metro systems have been expanded and modernised massively. It is now better connected, although links along the Mediterranean axis from North Africa to northern Europe need improving. The place quality of the city is extraordinarily good. From the Olympics onwards, it has made great efforts to improve the urban fabric, creating a place which is both modern but authentic with deep roots in its traditional culture and identity. And it has made huge efforts to develop and promote its image nationally, in Europe and globally. It has a powerful and successful economic development agency – Barcelona Activa. But social challenges are growing, and the global economic challenge is also greater.

Barcelona's experience has also underlined the importance of territorial governance. Its economic achievement in recent decades has almost been despite rather than because of the governance arrangements for the city-region area. Fragmentation and conflicts within the city-region area have led to unbalanced economic and social growth across the city and arguably to its economic underperformance. Barcelona City Council has demonstrated leadership and strategic decision-making capacity and has delivered many substantial projects. But since the abolition of the metropolitan agency in 1987, the governance of the wider Barcelona area has been a challenge. The fragmentation of local government has been a constraint upon the wider metropolitan area's economic development, even allowing for the success of a series of voluntary Metropolitan Strategic Plans, which encouraged wider working. It is very significant that a new Barcelona Metropolitan Agency was approved in 2010. But it is crucial that it has the powers and resources to help Barcelona to operate at a greater economic and geographic scale than it currently does. Working together at the increased scale of the real Barcelona urban economy – not artificial local government boundaries – is the key to the city-region's future economic performance and social development. To play on the world stage it needs the advantages that scale brings. That could be Barcelona's next "grand project".

There are challenges ahead for Barcelona city-region – economic, social and political. Unemployment has risen recently because of the global recession. The collapse of the housing market has left some with negative equity and the increased pressure upon existing stock has led to very high rentals. The pressure upon public expenditure, given the need to expand its infrastructure, is a challenge. The city has become much more ethnically diverse during the past decade with an increased number of city residents born outside Spain. This has brought many assets and benefits to the city. But increased social and economic challenges for all groups in a recession, especially recent immigrants, means Barcelona will have to pay particular attention to sustaining social cohesion in the next decade. Barcelona has demonstrated clear leadership. Nevertheless, some argue that the longevity of the political system which has been an advantage is becoming a liability as the new generation feels it cannot enter the political elite or the old model of development appropriate to an earlier period is no longer as relevant for the future.

Barcelona has again underlined the significance of national and more importantly regional policy for success. Democratisation and decentralisation of government and decision-making since 1979 has arguably increased the capacity of Catalonia and Barcelona metropolitan area as its key driver. However many in Barcelona feel that their success has been almost despite rather than because of national government policy. They argue that the primary focus of national policy is to support the capital

Madrid rather than other second tier cities in Spain. There is no coherent national urban strategy for Spain. Transport policy it has been argued is primarily designed to strengthen Madrid rather than second tier cities. The cities themselves have limited financial powers because so much of reform has been focused upon creating successful regional institutions rather than sub regional and urban institutions. In Barcelona there is a view that the city is still challenged by Madrid's economic dominance and that many decision-making powers and the headquarters of key firms have moved to the capital in recent years at the expense of Barcelona. There is pride in Barcelona's achievements against the odds. But there is also a great desire for a national strategy that would encourage its continued success.

Also, global competition will be fiercer in future. The city and the city government must continue to become more international, more multilingual, and more business friendly. Despite the improvements it has made in recent years, the city-region needs to improve its skills and innovation levels even further. Also, Barcelona must strive to fulfil its international ambitions without losing its authenticity and identity, which makes it so different and hence attractive to residents, visitors and investors. But Barcelona has recognised and is therefore well positioned to meet those challenges. Its economy is fundamentally sound. The investment it has made in both image and infrastructure endures. There is significant public-private sector consensus on what needs to be done. The city council is well managed with debt levels below some other Spanish cities. The city invested less in financial services and the property boom and has experienced less of a collapse. So it has a huge amount to work with. And despite the crisis, Barcelona is also better placed than most other Spanish cities to emerge intact because of its diversified economy, robust governance models, increasingly innovative economy, long term infrastructure investment, sound financial management and lack of over-dependence upon the finance and housing markets which have recently collapsed in many countries including Spain.

3.5 Richard Evans: Munich – local leadership drives performance in a decentralised system

Munich is one of Europe's most economically successful second tier cities. Its history, geography, economy and the German model of Federalism and local and regional governance are crucial to its success. It has many important assets but governance and political exploitation of them have been crucial and suggest lessons for other European second tier cities. Munich has excelled because of determined, visionary political leadership and because of integrated policy-making especially in innovation and infrastructure. But it is not immune from economic challenges and shares other cities' frustrations in developing effective governance across the city-region.

Germany is a good example of the relationship between governance and urban performance. It is not possible for other European countries to simply imitate the structural characteristics of the German system. Nevertheless, the key principles of the German experience can be transferred between different countries. It has the most decentralised policy-making system and also many of the highest performing cities in Europe. The system is not free from economic and social challenges and in particular is not free from very uneven development between West and East. Its approach to policy-making has important implications for the rest of Europe. Its key features are the levels of decentralisation, commitment to long-term planning and action, the allocation of powers to regional and urban authorities, the focus upon innovation, education, research and development. The German system has helped create one of the most balanced urban systems in Europe. Neither Berlin nor any of its second tier cities dominate in terms of population or economic performance. Berlin lags behind Germany's leading second tier cities in terms of its range of urban functions and overall economic performance but is now receiving considerable federal government investment.

The German economy is the strongest and most resilient in Europe. This is primarily because of its strong manufacturing industries and export base, overseas demand, restructuring of its national finances, national economic stimulus programmes, low wage inflation as well as avoidance of the real estate bubble because of its decentralised land markets, preference for rented rather than owner occupier housing and consequent lack of speculation. However, Germany's economic resilience has been helped by key state and city actors putting in place the necessary infrastructure and investment so that key urban economies flourish.

National policy has also been crucially important to the development of second tier cities. Many state capitals grew rapidly during the 40-year period when Bonn replaced Berlin as capital and gained key firms. Germany's decentralised system of governance has provided state and city governments with the powers and resources to improve cities' competitiveness. The federal government has also made heavy countercyclical investments to maintain the competitiveness of key sectors of the economy and cities. Cities have benefited from German technology policy which has prioritised long-term investment in research and education, skills programmes, diffusion of technology in key sectors, co-operation between academic institutions and businesses, promotion of technology start ups and research and technology based clusters. Policy-making is well integrated vertically and horizontally and based on negotiation and compromise. The policy of backing winners in the face of mounting international competition has pervaded all levels of government. Persistent focus on catering for private sector needs has also promoted close joint working between business, research organisations and governmental elites.

Munich, one of the most highly performing and successful of the German state capitals, has rapidly become a growth pole of European as well as Bavarian and German significance since the end of the Second World War. Munich city-region accounts for 29% of Bavaria's GDP and 21% of its population and 5.2% of Germany's GDP and 3.2% of its population. It is of even greater significance and importance in terms of its economic potential since it is a leading centre of innovation. Germany is Europe's strongest economy. The economic performance of Germany and its leading cities such as Munich will have a significant bearing on Europe's future prospects.

Munich is the capital city of a very large state with a population of over 12 million people. It is an exceptional kind of second tier city. Nevertheless, it tells us a great deal about the roots of urban success and has many messages for governments and partners at different government and territorial levels. Its experience confirms many of the key observations of this book. It clearly underlines the value of national strategies supporting high performing cities beyond the capital across its wider territory. It underlines the significance of local leadership and actions. It reinforces the significance of the key drivers of innovation, economic diversity, and place quality and strategic governance capacity. It underlines the importance of cities operating in wider circles – sub-regional, national, European and beyond. Munich offers a wealth of good practice in terms of policy-making. For example, its key actors have consistently pursued a set of coherent policies for supporting wealth creation, but never lost sight of social cohesion and environmental sustainability goals. They have invested heavily in new technology industries, technology transfer and innovation, physical infrastructure such as ICT and transport facilities, developed an excellent education system and promoted research and development organisations between academia and industry. Conscious policy decisions about urban form, conservation, tourism, arts and cultural facilities have also helped ensure it has good place quality. Cooperation and partnership working are intrinsic to Munich and Germany's governmental system and also the city's civic culture. The secrets of Munich's success are: good governance and networking; policy stability and continuity; intelligent interventions on the key drivers of competitiveness; a balanced approach to competitiveness, cohesion and environmental sustainability; a respect for the past, combined with a forward-looking mentality ("the Munich Way") and maintaining economic diversity (the "Munich Mix").

National policy has been crucially important to Munich's success. Germany's decentralised system of governance has provided state and city governments with the scope and financial capacity to strengthen the city's asset base and its competitiveness, especially after the Second World War and to later maintain it when it faced external threats in the early 1990s. Munich has also benefited from German technology policy given its concentration of HEIs and public research organisations and its dynamic, diverse economy.

The Munich experience underlines that creating local governance capacity is a complex process and the consequence of national and regional as well as local relationships. There is a strong tradition of networking between public and private sectors created by mutual interest, personnel with knowledge of partners' perspectives as well as by policy initiatives. High levels of autonomy have enabled both the state and city to implement far reaching policies relating to physical infrastructure and business support. Such capacity has also enabled both state and city governments to respond to any threats that the city might be overtaken by its rivals. The city established and retained arms' length companies to run key infrastructure such as the airport, public utilities, trade fairs and leisure facilities. Municipal enterprise has enabled strategic investment in key infrastructure and encouraged the growth of new industries, for example in the environmental technology sector. City government policies have also prioritised inclusiveness which has helped produce a relatively socially cohesive as well as successful city, despite significant pockets of poverty.

Munich in particular underlines the significance of innovation as a driver of success. It has pursued innovation longer and more systematically than most other European cities. The process involves many stakeholders within the state, the universities and the private sector. The partnerships are complex and overlapping and the process is self-reinforcing. Munich has a powerful culture of consensus between stakeholders and networks. Effective multi-level governance ensures that the weight of the federal government and land innovation programmes are brought to bear but also tailored and embedded because many of Munich's key research and business support organisations play a pivotal role in implementing these programmes. Munich's innovation system has grown incrementally and is characterised by continuity, institutional thickness, trust, cooperation, a complex web of relationships and supply of high level skills and is therefore deeply embedded within the city. Munich also has a vast knowledge base. Munich and the state of Bavaria have established a high quality education system and an infrastructure which supports the development of business and innovation. The constant expansion of the universities and the attraction of researchers from abroad and support for the development of a number of clusters laid the grounds for success. The universities have invested huge resources to improve the quality of research and to develop an entrepreneurial culture. The Chamber of Commerce is very powerful and plays an important role in involving small and medium-sized enterprises in the policy process and importing innovation into them.

Finally, Munich shows that territorial governance matters to economic performance. The most problematic issue facing Munich is city regional governance. Although the city is Germany's largest local authority, it is surrounded by many small municipalities. Rapid urban expansion has meant that many key businesses are located outside the city boundary and planning and transportation issues need to be handled on a city regional basis. There is no institutional means of ensuring that an integrated development strategy is adopted at a city-region level which can ensure that Munich expands in both an efficient and environmentally sustainable way. Success has come at a heavy environmental price. The large amount of low density development in areas without access to rapid transit is environmentally and physically unsustainable. Land and transportation planning, policy-making and implementation is very patchy and uneven because responsibility is so fragmented. Historic attempts by the city to extend its influence and boundaries have always been resisted by the surrounding municipalities.

Despite its economic success, Munich faces a number of challenges. It faces competition from other German cities and major cities outside Germany. German cities tend to be under-represented politically within federal or state governments and face fiscal pressures since responsibilities are not matched with the necessary resources. Munich is a relatively expensive place to live and operate a business. Land is cheaper, housing more affordable and business tax rates lower in surrounding municipalities and improvements in transport have made them more accessible. All this has prompted decentralisation of economic activity but also extensive in-commuting. As Munich has prospered and grown, the need to secure a coherent sub-regional approach to economic development, planning, and governance and policy-making has become ever more pressing. Weak city regional governance could damage Munich's longer term prospects since the present rate of land consumption and traffic growth cannot continue indefinitely without causing severe congestion, environmental degradation, associated diseconomies such as delays in journeys to work and supply of goods, deteriorating quality of life and ultimately strangulation.

3.6 Richard Meegan: Leeds – innovative strategic governance and local leadership

Until relatively recently, England had an urban policy but no real policy for cities. There has been an explicit urban policy for over forty years – primarily concerned with welfare issues and addressing the social, economic and environmental impact of economic restructuring on cities. It was not until the end of the 1990s that what could be described as a "cities policy" began to take shape. The Labour government had two strands to its urban policy. The first strengthened the focus on social inclusion and neighbourhood renewal. The second was an embryonic cities policy in which cities were seen as places of economic dynamism and "renaissance". Reinforcing this central government shift was the initiative of cities themselves in promoting their development potential and importance to the national economy. In England this saw the formation of the Core Cities Group, which brings together the local authorities of the eight largest second tier cities to promote their joint development interests. In England, Urban Regeneration Companies (URCs) were also set up to take responsibility for the physical regeneration of designated areas in a number of second-tier cities. Policy was also influenced by government attempts to modernise local government with city authorities encouraged, for example, to work in partnership with other agencies and local communities through Local Strategic Partnerships (LSPs); an approach further reinforced by the introduction of Local Area Agreements (LAAs) where public sector partners were encouraged to combine spending programmes to meet local targets agreed with government. City-regional partnerships were also promoted to provide governance at the level of functional economic areas, accompanied by matching Multi-Area Agreements (MAAs) across local authority boundaries. The panoply of LSPs, LAAs, MAAs and city-regional partnerships demonstrated both the degree to which local development was increasingly being delivered through multi-level collaborative governance and an implicit, if not explicit, recognition on the part of government of the need for some form of devolution of powers.

The Conservative-Liberal Democrat coalition government set in train a major shift in policy away from regional economic development to a more localist approach in which the setting up of sub-regional Local Enterprise Partnerships has been encouraged. The government made it clear that its immediate priorities were deficit reduction and its localism agenda for encouraging growth. It did not intend to produce a national regeneration strategy or framework as it saw this as being inconsistent with its localism agenda. It is up to local partners to identify their own regeneration priorities and strategies using a "toolkit" of devolved powers, flexibilities and government funding incentives and support programmes. It is under the banner of *"Unlocking Growth in Cities"* that a policy for second tier cities might emerge. Powers over regeneration, housing, transport and broadband infrastructure, skills, rates and local revenue raising are being devolved through negotiated "city deals", initially with the eight English core cities and their wider Local Enterprise Partnerships, but eventually extending to other cities.

Leeds acts as an important counterweight to London and the South East in the national economy. Outside of the capital, it is first in employment for printing, construction, financial and business services and knowledge-based industries; second for manufacturing, distribution hotels and restaurants and personal services; and third for legal, creative and digital and transport and communications industries. It has successfully hosted public sector jobs transferred from the capital, strengthening in the process its regional administrative role. The city-region has the second largest functional sub-national economy after the capital, accounting for around 5% of the national economy. It is a major economic centre yet still not exhibiting some of the agglomeration diseconomies of the capital. And, importantly, the polycentric structure of both the city and city-region means it has the potential to grow further.

The city's powers are relatively limited in the UK's unitary state system. It finds itself on the receiving end of an often rapidly changing array of policies from central government departments and national agencies that it needs to join together at local level. A distinctive response to that political and policy context has been the city's partnership-based approach to place-making in the shape of the "Leeds Initiative", which has produced a series of "visions" for the development of the city. Initially focused on economic development, the remit of the "Leeds Initiative" has been extended to social and environmental concerns and its membership has also widened from the public and private sectors to include the third sectors. Would the city have been more successful if there had been more decentralisation of powers? The politicians and policy-makers interviewed argued strongly that more devolved powers would have helped the city's economic development.

The city has not been eligible for major levels of European or national regional policy funding but the policies that it has been able to secure have had significant impact. The Urban Development Corporation did act as a catalyst for waterfront regeneration that the council and Leeds Initiative were able to build on. And national urban policy has assisted the regeneration of priority areas. This support, however, has been sporadic and time-limited so, for some key schemes, there has had to be a continual juggling of funding to maintain momentum.

National policies for innovation, skills and connectivity have been important in the city's development, albeit with mixed outcomes. The Leeds initiative and the city-region have put major efforts into developing innovation strategies, emphasising industrial collaboration and the transfer of university expertise to industry. But the city has not been helped by the absence at national level of a coherent regionalised industrial and innovation policy. A regional dimension to national innovation policy was provided, for a time, by the Regional Development Agency, Yorkshire Forward, which did support a number of university-based innovation projects in the city-region. But this spatial dimension to innovation policy has been lost with the agency's abolition. Nationally-financed universities and further education institutions are key city assets. And Leeds has engaged over time with all the various national skills agencies to develop its own skills and children and young people strategies. But the "top-down" nature of this relationship explains the city-region's "ask" for more devolved powers in skills development policies as part of the "city deal" it is negotiating with the government. National skills policies need to be grounded at local level and the city needs more powers to achieve this.

National government support has been particularly problematic in relation to transport. Leeds has been successful in securing national funding for road building. It has struggled, however, with its public transport infrastructure, which has become a key issue as road congestion has worsened. The failure to secure central government funding for a light rail transit system provides a classic example of both central government control of transport infrastructure investments and the limited local revenue raising powers of local government to compensate for this. It also highlighted the large and growing gap between transport spending in London and the rest of the country and points, more generally, to the need for greater transparency in the territorial distribution of public spending.

The city began exploring city-region links and relationships a number of years before central government actively promoted the idea. It has successfully developed city-regional institutions and policies, culminating in the establishment of the city-region Local Enterprise Partnership. The city-region's functional economic rationale and appropriateness for infrastructure development and key policies like innovation and skills have local political support. But this support needs to be nurtured and adequately resourced and this remains a challenging task. It is not helped by the absence of a national regeneration framework and the dismantling of the intermediate regional planning and economic development frameworks that were put in place over the past decade.

A fundamental challenge facing the city and city-region is the impact of the recession. Forecasts are for a relatively slow and protracted recovery. Combined with continuing population growth, this raises difficult questions about the ability of the city's economy to provide enough jobs. Employment in the city has fallen back to the level reached a decade ago and unemployment has risen in both the city and city-region. The growth of the 2000s was not equally shared and was accompanied by the development of a "two-speed city" that has been the focus of policies aimed at "narrowing the gap". There is a real danger that this gap will widen further as a result of the recession.

Leeds has recognised that the recession and wider environmental issues underline the need for a new growth model and has produced a growth strategy that has more of a sustainable development emphasis. It aims to build, for example, on the diversity of the financial and business services sector by identifying new opportunities such as low carbon and environmental investment. And it has a strong focus on low carbon growth identifying opportunities in Leeds' manufacturing sector and in housing and construction with, for example, the retrofitting of social housing. The health and medical sector and the city's growing creative and digital industries are also targeted for growth and the need for support for social enterprise and the third sector is recognised. This sustainable development focus also runs through the Local Enterprise Partnership's development plan for the city-region.

Leeds would be helped in its post-recession strategy for growth by a national policy framework that involves genuine devolution of powers as part of a broader programme for re-balancing the economy. Whether the current government's proposals for devolving powers to cities through its "city deals" amount to such a policy remains to be seen. But they are a step in this direction.

4   The basic features of place leadership

In this chapter, to better understand generative leadership, input is sought from all available forms of territorially-oriented leadership studies including place, regional, city, rural, and also cluster leadership. These different types of studies are not defined clearly in the literature, and they overlap in many ways and the concepts are often used interchangeably. Thus, it would be an exaggeration to say that they form clear schools of thought. Rather, they are found in individual publications referring to both different and similar patterns of leadership – here they are placed under the generic rubric of place leadership. The rationale of stretching our search beyond city leadership to cover somewhat different spatial contexts is that this allows us to identify the key dimensions of generative leadership in urban and regional development for further scrutiny. What the many studies on place leadership vividly illustrate is how a new order of leadership emerges with new modes of governance and networks. They challenge some of the basic assumptions of organisationally oriented leadership literature and confirm others. They also show that, in spite of visible differences in the context, there are several similarities between, say, cities, rural areas and clusters, and even countries, as they all are complex social entities, and as leadership is fundamentally about human interaction. In these respects, the differences between countries and different spatial scales may not be as great as we like to think, even though they clearly exist, as was shown in Chapter 3. But of course, nuanced comparative analyses are likely to reveal that underneath the generic similarities, there are grassroots differences in the ways place leaders mobilise themselves and other actors. Earlier studies have shown that leadership in places is indeed identifiable, and that the practices may vary substantially in and across places while meeting similar generic needs. They also show "a place" is a unique constellation in which to study leadership (e.g. Horlings, 2012a and 2012b; Collinge and Gibney, 2010a; Bailey *et al.*, 2010; Blazek, 2013).

Just as city and regional economic development is "path-dependent" (Martin and Sunley 2006) and rooted in socio-economic and cultural contexts, so is place leadership itself (MacNeill and Steiner, 2010; Kostiainen and Sotarauta, 2003; Beer and Baker, 2012). The past trajectories of a specific place, moulded by socio-economic-political incidents and events, shape local cultures and thus also the local understanding of leaders and their leadership styles: they frame what is appropriate and what is not. The place leadership literature recognises complexity in the ways leadership is expressed and enacted – it may be more centralised or distributed, and fragmented or shared in its nature. Collinge and Gibney (2011) say that actors, human beings, continuously construct and reconstruct the physical, socio-economic, cultural and political dimension of the places in which they live and work, and in turn they are shaped by the very same places. For these reasons, in place leadership, "a spatial literacy of place is required" (Trickett and Lee, 2010: 434). Drawing on Cresswell (2004), Collinge *et al.* (2011) identify three basic senses of place: (a) location, which is the fixed geographical coordinates of a precise physical location; (b) locale, which is the idea of place considered as the material setting for social relations; and (c) the sense of place, which is the subjective emotional attachment people have to places they inhabit (Collinge and Gibney, 2011; Cresswell, 2004). Additionally, as Horlings (2012b) shows us, there are place leaders who are not motivated solely by their own private interests but who have strong feelings for the place and/or the target of their development efforts.

Place leadership is concerned with (a) facilitating interdisciplinary development strategies and practices across institutional boundaries, technology themes and professional cultures and (b) ensuring the comprehensive engagement of various communities so that they are able to contribute to and benefit from the development processes and their outcomes (Gibney *et al.*, 2009; Gollinge and Gibney, 2011). Thus, in line with governance thinking, generative leadership in a city, a form of place leadership, is by its very nature distributed. The competences, resources and powers needed are distributed in city development among many actors instead of only one or few. This should be seen giving great potential to the economic development of cities. In this kind of setting, leaders often lead without formal power, and they need to span their own spheres of influence and operational boundaries by generating and tapping into networks, and also by drawing on and working alongside a range of different stakeholders. As Liddle (2003) points out, also formally assigned leaders often work beyond traditional boundaries in uncharted territories with state, non-state, business and auxiliary organisations that are ill-defined and poorly networked, and which have imprecise boundaries and role ambiguities. Liddle (2012: 37) argues further that in the future, "leaders must continually move beyond their own organisational boundaries into collaborative leadership spaces and act on behalf of the city-region for the public interest", and it is the generative leaders who create collaborative spaces.

In distributed settings, place leaders need to represent their organisations and also places more broadly (Gibney, 2011b). McNeill and Steiner (2010) put it differently; they say that place leaders need to obtain involvement and "buy-in" from wide range economic actors. Conversely, they also need to involve other actors in their own development efforts. Gibney (2011) raises the distributed leadership bar even higher by calling for leadership approaches that "can think and move beyond the 'them versus us' or 'me versus them' leitmotifs that are embedded in competitively oriented leadership prescriptions". As many actors participate in and contribute to development efforts with their own incentives, logics, drivers and paymasters, it may be difficult to find the boundaries of generative leadership or common ground, as situations change over time and different policy areas present challenges that call for different actors to take the lead (Norman, 2013).

In the place leadership literature, the primary emphasis often is on formal leadership, which refers to the deliberate coordination of followers in the pursuit of a consciously espoused goals and that places leadership within the purposive strand of governance (Collinge and Gibney, 2010b). Of course, by definition, leaders enjoy a higher status and/or a more central position relative to others in terms of their contributions to the place in question; however, as Norman (2013) points out, formal place leadership, and thus also formal authority, plays a less significant role than it does in leadership theories for formal organisations. It is evident that leadership practices regarding how much development efforts revolve around formal leadership vary between governance systems and to some degree also within them. What is undeniable is that formal leaders dealing with city development are faced with a wider range of actors than previously, and the many networks are seasoned with more varied mixes of global, national and local players as well as increased technical complexity. All this means that they need to involve knowledge that is dispersed and disparate across partners and rivals (Gibney, 2011b). These are the reasons why leaders are increasingly called on to stimulate and lead change agendas without having the formal power but with the responsibility to generate something new. If the distributed assets can be mobilised to serve both joint and individual needs, it may be possible to forge a collaborative dynamic development effort, which is something more than an individual actor can demonstrate alone.

So, distributed place leadership is an emergent property of interacting individuals (Bennett *et al.*, 2003), and hence, the subject and object of agency regarding who leaders and followers are may vary (Huxham and Vangen, 2000). For these reasons, place leadership conceives that generative leaders should understand the logic of issue-based development processes and continuously endeavour to transcend the inward-looking aims of the various organisations and to find "third solutions" that would benefit the future development of an entire city instead of a selected few, and simultaneously also promote individual interests and objectives. Therefore, place leadership is likely to focus on activities like motivating, involving, empowering, supporting, sense-making, mobilising, controlling, manipulating, legitimising and representing – activities that are on the surface not so very different from leadership executed in organisational contexts (Sydow *et al.*, 2011). In line with the contemporary leadership literature, place leadership is more useful when seen as an activity instead of an individual in possession of a formal position. Thus, place leadership is the generative force that causes goals to be met and found and missions to be accomplished in a place rather than a formally constructed institutional position in a governance structure. Place development calls for leaders who are able to:

- Lead by a process of influence, reconciling competing and conflicting interests;

- Lead collaborative advantage, understanding of the challenges associated with transforming places as well as organisations;
- Operate with and through ever-changing relational processes in place and time, and hence often leading without formal power, and also leading other leaders;
- Understand the interface between different spatial scales and the intended and unintended consequences of a given intervention;
- Lead and work effectively within constantly changing policy environments, and thus have an understanding of how cross-sector synergies and resources can be brought to bear in the shaping of place; and
- Bend mainstream resources and attract benefits in kind to draw in sufficient resources to "make it happen".

(Trickett and Lee, 2010: 434)

Leadership and the act of leading is what leaders in their manifold ways do, but the tendency to conflate leadership with authority and formal power may still overshadow some important aspects of it. This is quite natural, as there often is a tendency to simplify the complex reality so that it becomes more understandable. It is tempting to address mainly assigned leadership by focusing on influential individuals with authority and formal positions, or to analyse the structure and processes of a city government. All this is visible, while non-assigned leaders and emergent forms of leadership are much more difficult to identify. Assigned leaders have a formal position and they are granted the authority to exercise power on behalf of some collectivity, while non-assigned leaders gain their leadership position without having a formal position because of the ways other people respond to them. Non-assigned leaders seize the power in spite of their lack of institutional and/or resource power (see Chapter 5).

The group of assigned leaders may include mayors and the chief executives of local/regional economic development agencies, and other leaders of organisations whose mission it is to boost the economic development of cities. Assigned leaders have an organisation, resources and/or a mandate to work for a city, while non-assigned leaders exercise other forms of influence, as their institutional position does not allow them any specific resources with which to make a difference. In place leadership, however, the boundary between assigned and non-assigned leadership is not at all clear. An assigned leader may become non-assigned when they aim to reach actors beyond those institutional arrangements from which the assignment is derived. Conversely, a non-assigned leader may gain authority if they can earn the respect of other actors, and/or if the institutional conditions change, thus enabling the leader to become an assigned leader.

Non-assigned leaders aim to make a difference by influencing the actors with power and resources, who, for their part, have a mandate and resources to boost economic development, and hence they may influence directly. As said, more often than not assigned leaders also need to work through, with and by other actors. But, we face another question: are all the assigned leaders actually real leaders? Like Samuels (2003), we are interested in leadership that aims to transform a city and leaves a legacy. Both assigned and non-assigned leaders may have a transformational effect that is acknowledged, but it is also possible that assigned leadership may leave no trace at all. Reflecting back to Tolstoyan notions of leadership, we can now say that place leadership develops along an axis in which the other extreme is a situation where the leader is dominant and exercises control over followers on the basis of some authority that she or he has over the other actors (Collinge and Gibney, 2010). If the dominance of assigned leaders is at one extreme, we can find non-assigned leaders who are dominant at the other extreme. It may even be the case that non-assigned leaders are able to select leadership objectives and priorities that assigned leaders make visible through their channels, but whose content they do not influence much (see Chapter 6). We can now distinguish three types of place leaders and their followers:

1. Assigned leaders who have a formal position in an organisation that is supposed one way or another to boost the economic development of a city but who mainly influence according to the mandate they possess and instruments that they have in their organisation. **These leaders lead their own organisations and influence wider networks through them** – they do what they are supposed to do, and they lead mainly followers assigned to them in their own organisations.
2. Assigned leaders who have a formal position in an organisation that is supposed one way or another to boost the economic development of a city but who actively reach beyond the body that has authorised them to influence broader spheres of influence. **These leaders lead their own organisations but they also aim to influence actors beyond their formal assignment** – they do what they are supposed to do but they also consciously aim to exercise influence by, with and through other actors.
3. Non-assigned leaders who do not have a formal role in boosting city development but who are willing and able to take leadership positions in wider networks of influence. **These leaders have neither an assignment nor a formal position to draw on or organisational resources at their disposal, and they do what they are not supposed to do but what they feel needs to be done.**

Generative leadership is a complex process that takes place between assigned and non-assigned leaders (Figure 4.1), leading us to ask: if leadership is distributed,

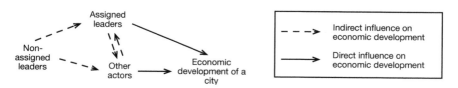

Figure 4.1 The conceptual relationships between assigned and non-assigned leaders with other actors and the economic development of a city.

and if there are several assigned and non-assigned leaders leading development games, who then are leaders and who are the followers? In leadership studies, it is generally assumed that leaders know who their followers are and followers know who is supposed to lead them. In generative leadership in cities, this is not the case; the relationship between leaders and followers is indeed ambiguous. As Sydow *et al.* (2011) observe, one of the main dilemmas is that there is a critical need for some kind of leadership, but that neither individual nor organisational actors wish to be led. As they suggest, this paradox can only be "managed" by organising for leading in a way that takes into account the tensions and contradictions surrounding leadership in complex social entities. This is exactly what this book aims to do. Table 4.1 reflects on the place leadership discussion in Chapter 3, and issues related to governance by simplifying the ways leadership is expressed in government and governance constellations.

Table 4.1 Place leadership in government and governance structures simplified

	Leadership in government	*Generative leadership in governance*
Core of the leadership	Assigned individual and/or group with a formal position	Distributed influence networks and influential individuals with an influence on each other
Nature of leadership	Control, directive	Generative, emergent
Source of influence	Position, authority	Role, behaviour, earned
Mobilisation	Transactional	Relational, transformative
Orientation	Top-down	Circular (simultaneously top-down, bottom-up and horizontal)
Followers	Pre-set, fairly stable	Emergent, changing
Objectives	Assumed to be relatively clear	Multiple, potentially conflicting
Access to resources	Direct	Indirect, and to some extent also direct

5   Power and leadership

5.1 Framing the concept of power

The emphasis on mobilisation, pooling and networks necessitates that generative leaders not only move outside their traditional departmental boundaries but also that they engage with a wide range of power relations among firms, and with many different types of actors each from their own fields, cultures and spatial scales of operation (Koppenjan and Klijn, 2004). While pushing towards something new, generative leaders are required to deal with the potential clashes of different institutional cultures and agendas and asymmetric power relationships (Burfitt and MacNeill, 2008). Generative leadership is not only about generating new networks and structures for innovation, but is also about social uncertainty and ambiguity. Changing the playground meddles with social relationships and power structures; thus, uncertainty is inherent. As Gibney (2012: 616) says, "leadership of uncertainty requires leaders to both have an appetite for risk and to be risk-aware; but to guide responses/solutions in the context of many unknowns". At the day-to-day level, increased uncertainty calls for humility and a willingness to be proved wrong and work with uncertainty (Gibney, 2012). For all these reasons, as Beer and Baker (2012) emphasise, any discussion of place leadership inevitably raises questions of power and the ability to influence either other actors within or external to a city. Generative leaders need to pool different sources of power and ways of exercising it. To understand generative leadership, we need to understand how different sources of power come together in networks to influence city development. Interestingly, in this kind of setting, power is not only a cause of leadership but also a consequence of it. If, and only if, followers follow, leaders become truly powerful (Riggio *et al.*, 2008).

The concept of power is among the key concepts in social sciences, with its several dimensions and definitions (cf. Wrong, 1997). There is a rich array of ways in which to conceptualise and study it. Drawing on Wrong (1997: 2), power can be defined as "the capacity of some persons to produce intended and foreseen effects on others". Wrong (1997) points out that the intentionality and effectiveness of power need to be scrutinised in order to fully understand the link between power and influence. Dahl's (2005) well-known approach to power reflects this premise. He sees power as amounting to control of the behaviour of other actors. So, when an actor A is able to break the resistance of an actor B (i.e. to cause B to do something they would not otherwise do), A is able to make the target act as he/she wants in spite of the will of B (see also Paloheimo and Wiberg, 2005.) Ideally, in generative leadership, A is able to induce B, C, D and so on to willingly do things they would not otherwise do.

Lukes (1986) challenges the intentionality of power, and asks whether power is actually the production of intended effects, as Dahl (2005) and Russell (1986) also seem to indicate. Lukes (1986: 1) asks, "would it not be possible to exercise power without deliberately aiming to do so?". In addition to unintentional effects, persuasion, requests, persuasive pieces of advice and/or convincing arguments ought to be included in the elaboration of power (Lukes, 1986; Wrong, 1997). As Foucault (1980) and Parsons (1986) famously note, the power of social systems and structures are also essential elements in the studies of power. Foucault (1980) maintains that, "power is everywhere . . . because it comes from everywhere". He speaks about covert power that works through people rather than only on them. Foucault claims that belief systems gain power when groups of people accept a belief system and take it for granted. These belief systems define the arena for many actors, affect institutional design and are often institutions in themselves (Foucault, 1980). Innes and Booher (2000) argue that the old forms of power are fading away because the interests that hold networks and dominant beliefs in them are increasingly diversified, and according to Castells (1997: 359) "the new power lies in the codes of information and in the images of representation around which societies organise their institutions and people build their lives and decide their behaviour". Allen (2003) rejects the idea of power flows but not networked relationships of power, and sees power as the relational effect of social interaction (Allen, 2003).

In a way, Lukes (2005) links the more straightforward views on power to Foucauldian notions of power by seeing it as a three-level entity. The first view (one-dimensional) contains behaviour, decision-making, key issues, observable conflict and (subjective) interests that are seen as policy preferences revealed by political participation. The first view is a measure of the outcomes of decisions, and hence the focus is on the behaviour in the decision-making on issues where there is a conflict of interest. The second view (two-dimensional) is based on a qualified critique of the behavioural focus. It adds non-decision-making, potential issues, observable (overt or covert) conflict and (subjective) interests that are seen as policy preferences or grievances. The second view differs from the first because it also acknowledges the ways in which decisions are prevented from being made on *potential* issues over which there is a conflict of interest. The third view (three-dimensional) includes, in addition to decision-making, the control over the political agenda (not necessarily through decisions), issues and potential issues, observable (overt or covert) and latent conflict, and subjective and real interests (Lukes, 2005: 29). The third view stresses that shaping preferences via values, norms and ideologies is a form of power too, and that all social interaction involves power because ideas operate behind all language and action. The third view includes those ideas or values that ground all social, political and religious ideals. All the features of the third view easily become routine and therefore actors do not consciously "think" of them. This is the way in which political ideologies inform policy-making without being explicit (Lukes, 2005), and this may be the reason why much city development activity is aimed at shaping institutions, networks and interpretations, that is, those factors that shape economic development without most of us even noticing it.

The combined effect of Lukes' (2005) three dimensions may be realised by the way that power blurs the dividing line between rationality and rationalisation, and manifests itself as highly context-dependent, as shown by Flyvbjerg (1998). Rationality is penetrated by power, and therefore, as Flyvbjerg maintains, rationalisation presented as rationality is often a principal strategy in the exercise of power. The front may be open to public scrutiny, but backstage, hidden from public view, power and rationalisation dominate, and there the forms of power raised in Lukes' third dimension may be consciously constructed and utilised. This kind of rationalised and socially and conveniently constructed front does not necessarily imply dishonesty. It is not unusual to find individuals, organisations and whole societies actually believing their own rationalisations (Flyvbjerg, 1998).

In their classic study of power, social psychologists French and Raven (1959) categorise power into five different bases or resources that power holders may rely upon. They divide later expert power into two modes of power, that is, informational and expert power. Although this categorisation is based on organisation-level analysis conducted decades ago in a different time and context, it still offers a useful framework for contemplation.

- **Legitimate power** – The power of an individual based on the relative position and duties of the holder of the position within an organisation. Formal authority is delegated to the holder of the position.
- **Referent power** – The power (or ability) of individuals to attract others and build loyalty, based on the charisma and interpersonal skills of the power holder.
- **Expert power** (this type of power is further broken down next into the further category of information power) – An individual's power is derived from the skills or expertise of the person and the organisation's needs for those skills and expertise. Unlike the other powers, this type of power is usually highly specific, and is limited to the particular area in which the expert is trained and qualified.
- **Information power** – People with this type of power are well-informed, up-to-date and also have the ability to persuade others. The difference between expert power and information power is subtle. One difference may be that people with expert power are perceived as exhibiting credibility through their image as having expertise (i.e. a qualified doctor in a doctor's uniform), while one with information power does not have a strict need to "look the part of a professional"; however, they must keep up-to-date with latest knowledge in their field, and have confidence in debating or in persuasion.

- **Reward power** – This mode of power depends upon the ability of the power wielder to confer valued material rewards. It refers to the degree to which the individual can give others a reward of some kind. This power is obvious, but also ineffective if abused.
- **Coercive power** – This form of power means the application of negative influences on employees. It might refer to the ability to demote or to withhold other rewards. It is the desire for valued rewards or the fear of having them withheld that ensures the obedience of those working under the power. Coercive power tends to be the most obvious, but least effective, form of power, as it builds resentment and resistance within its targets.

(French and Raven, 1959; adapted from Wikipedia, 26 June 2008)

5.2 Power and forms of leadership in local and regional economic development – empirical evidence from Finland

Power is a potential to influence; it is a latent resource that needs to be freed and utilised by means of other processes. Influence is here defined as a process by which the generative leaders, drawing on their latent resources by interaction skills and other social skills, make other actors see things, people, functions and so on differently from before, and as a result do something that they would not otherwise do. In any case, local generative leaders need power to influence, but the question is, what kind of power?

Drawing from both extensive survey (see Appendix 1) and interview data[1], this chapter focuses on the forms of leadership and resources used for the exercise of power of Finnish local and regional development officers. In this study, both assigned and non-assigned place leaders as well as local and regional development officers without any leadership position were interviewed and responded to the survey. The main result was that whatever position the actors possessed, they believed that they needed to take leadership in their own operational environments to produce results. Those local/regional development officers who did not enjoy leadership positions but worked to achieve such a position could be labelled as aspirational generative leaders. The empirical study clearly shows that local and regional development champions stress the indirect methods of influencing, and this confirms the view on city development opened up by the concepts of governance and influence networks. Most of the respondents (94.5%) regarded the construction of an atmosphere of trust as an important way to influence other actors, and hence also economic development. If trust was highly stressed, so was organising capacity, as 89.6% of the respondents stressed the importance of organising development work and its influence networks more efficiently. Taken together, all the influence tactics regarded as important were, in one way or another, indirect in nature: strategy work, influencing communication and removing obstacles to it, and acting as a role model were also emphasised by most of the respondents. What is interesting is that various institutional and direct ways to exert influence were not seen as being as important as the more indirect leadership tactics. According to the survey, Finnish local and regional development champions do not rely much on delegating their own responsibilities to the other actors. They did not generally see provocation, invoking the regional development acts and/or development programmes, or the sense of responsibility of the key decision-makers as important means of influence.

In the institutional promotion of city development, Lukes' (1986) two first views of power are usually emphasised whereby the policy institutions value powers to act and decide, as well as the design of new institutions and strategies. The interview and survey data indicate, however, that from the generative leader's point of view inducing is a more important tactic than the straightforward formulation of strategies, not to mention coercion. Generative leaders see local and regional development as a subtle process, essential to which is the renewal of behavioural models, attitudes and beliefs. Their view, based on their own experience, is rather Foucauldian in nature and stresses clearly Lukes' third view. Generative leaders use many different kinds of influence tactics, but first and foremost they rely on communication, interaction and social skills. Figure 5.1 provides us with a view of the influence tactics that actual and aspirational place leaders regarded as important in their work.

To gain a more focused view the survey data was grouped, and four new sum variables were constructed. These are network leadership, institutional leadership, interpretive leadership and strategic leadership. They were first of all identified by content analysis of the interview data and were then verified by confirmatory

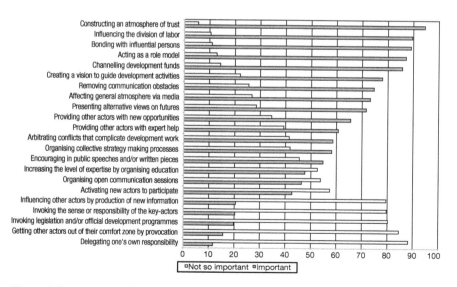

Figure 5.1 Answers to the question: "Assess, based on your own experiences, what measures are important in the efforts to influence other actors in the name of local/regional development?" (%) (n = 526 to 531).

factor analysis (see also, Sotarauta *et al.*, 2007). The new sum variables to measure influence tactics and core variables included in the new variables were constructed as follows (the sum variables are renamed here to better reflect their leadership qualities) (cf. Sotarauta, 2009):

- **Network leadership**
    - constructing an atmosphere of trust;
    - arbitrating conflicts that complicate development work;
    - removing communication obstacles between actors;
    - organising development work so that the roles of individual actors are clear; and
    - bonding with influential persons.

- **Institutional leadership**
    - invoking legislation and/or official development programmes; and
    - invoking the sense of responsibility of the key actors.

- **Interpretive leadership**
    - encouraging other actors in public speeches and written pieces;
    - presenting alternative views on futures, and the promotion of regional development, thus influencing other actors;
    - influencing other actors by the production of new information; and
    - affecting the general atmosphere via the media.

- **Strategic leadership**
    - creating a vision to guide the development activities of several actors; and
    - organising collective strategy making processes.

These new sum variables[2] clearly show how both actual and aspirational generative leaders appreciate indirect forms of leadership more than direct ones (see Figure 5.2).

What is striking is the fact that it is not possible to find statistically significant differences between the four forms of leadership or influence tactics and regions and cities, organisation types, seniority and position in one's own organisation. In Finland, generative leaders are surprisingly unanimous about how to influence. There are no international studies on these issues that would provide this study with comparative observations.

The survey data shows that the Finnish actual and aspirational generative leaders consider information and networks are their most important resources used for the exercise of power (see Figure 5.2). Actual and aspirational generative leaders stressed that networks are both resources of new information and an important support factor in putting various ideas and initiatives through decision-making processes. The next most important resource of power was such expert information that enables generative leaders to not only convince decision-makers of the

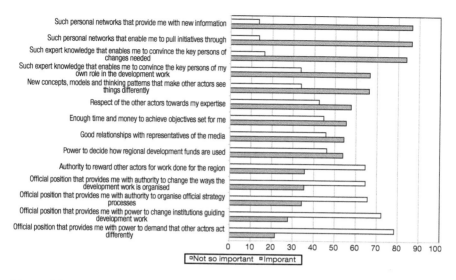

Such personal networks that provide me with new information
Such personal networks that enable me to pull initiatives through
Such expert knowledge that enables me to convince the key persons of changes needed
Such expert knowledge that enables me to convince the key persons of my own role in the development work
New concepts, models and thinking patterns that make other actors see things differently
Respect of the other actors towards my expertise
Enough time and money to achieve objectives set for me
Good relationships with representatives of the media
Power to decide how regional development funds are used
Authority to reward other actors for work done for the region
Official position that provides me with authority to change the ways the development work is organised
Official position that provides me with authority to organise official strategy processes
Official position that provides me with power to change institutions guiding development work
Official position that provides me with power to demand that other actors act differently

0 10 20 30 40 50 60 70 80 90 100

□Not so important ▫Imporant

Figure 5.2 Answers to the statement: "Assess what factors are important in your own work when you try to influence other actors in the name of local/regional development" (%) (n = from 526 to 531).

importance of the required changes, but also of the personal role in the development process of the actors themselves. The most important resources used for the exercise of power support the above view that the leadership is indirect in nature. Direct sources of power such as an official institutional position, a power to make changes to institutions governing the development activities, or an official position in designing regional development strategies and/or development programmes were not seen as particularly important.

Figure 5.3 provides us with a view of the resources used for the exercise of power that both actual and aspirational generative leaders regard as important in their efforts to influence the actors for local/regional development. As with forms of leadership (influence tactics), a more focused view on the sources of power was achieved by grouping the data and creating four new sum variables: interpretive power, network power, institutional power and resource power. They were identified in the same way as they were in the case of influence tactics. The new sum variables measuring resources used for the exercise of power and the variables that make up the new variables are as follows:

- **Institutional power**

  - official position that provides me with power to demand that other actors act differently;
  - official position that provides me with power to change institutions guiding development work;

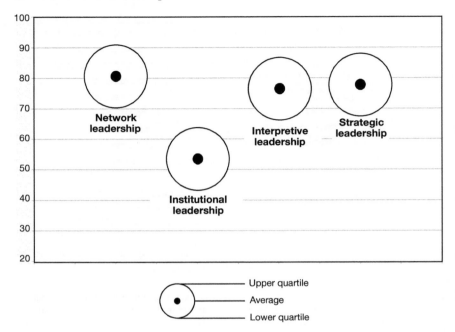

Figure 5.3 Stylised illustration of the four sub-types of generative leadership (n = 531)

- official position that provides me with authority to organise official strategy processes; and
- official position that provides me with authority to change the ways the development work is organised.

- **Interpretive power**
    - such expert knowledge that enables me to convince the key persons of the changes needed;
    - new concepts, models and thinking patterns that make other actors see things differently; and
    - such expert knowledge that enables me to convince the key persons of my own role in the development work.

- **Resource power**
    - power to decide how regional development funds are used;
    - authority to reward other actors for work done for the region; and
    - enough time and money to achieve objectives set for me.

- **Network power**
    - such personal networks that enable me to push initiatives through;
    - respect of the other actors for my expertise;

– good relationships with representatives of the media; and
– such personal networks that provide me with new information.

The most important forms of power that generative leaders need are interpretive power and network power. The median of both of these forms of power is 80.0, and most of the respondents considered these to be the most important forms of power in their own work. Interpretive power was regarded as being slightly more important than network power. The average for the sum variable measuring interpretive power is 82.4, while in the case of network power it is 77.7. The average of resource power is 66.7, and institutional power is low at 58.0. Local and regional development officers were fairly unanimous in that the possibilities of affecting other actors' thinking and networking exceeded resources and institutions in importance (Figure 5.4). As with influence tactics, it was not possible to find statistically significant differences in resources used for the exercise of power between regions, organisation types, seniority and position in one's own organisation.

This categorisation of powers differs somewhat from the categorisation of French and Raven (1959). Institutional power is a combination of legitimate power and reward power, but not coercive power. The interviewees unanimously shared the view that any effort of coercion only leads to their exclusion from membership of all the important influence networks. Interpretive power is closely linked to

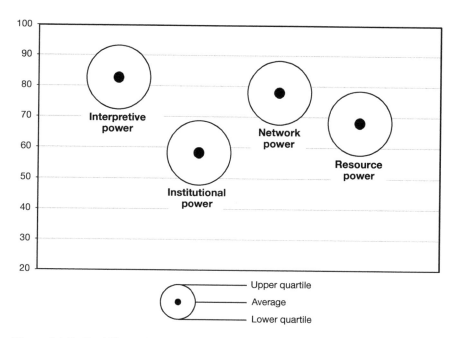

Figure 5.4 Stylised illustration of the generic forms of power and their importance in the work of local and regional development officers

information power, but highlights the importance of creating new mind-sets and ways of seeing various issues. Expertise power and referent power are not separately raised here, but they were extensively discussed in the interviews. They are scarce resources among place leaders, and the interviewees saw that expertise and referent power are the outcomes of the four sets of power raised here. French and Raven (1959) did not mention network power, but in the early twenty-first century it emerged as highly important and can be interpreted as one dimension in a wide debate about new modes of governance.

In sum, this Chapter suggests that if generative leaders master the four forms of power – network, institutional, resource and interpretive – and find their style of leadership, they may become truly influential. But, it is uncommon for one person to master all four, and therefore, the four forms of power need to be seen from an influence network perspective. If generative leaders seek to be influential, they need to be able to integrate the four main forms of power and channel them through different types of influence networks to promote knowledge city development.

5.3 Power and influence networks

Coordination, mobilisation and hence also the selective activation of the actors with important resources, competencies, power and knowledge are among the core tasks in any generative leader's activity. Therefore, it has been argued that actors who are able to enrol others in networks are particularly important. The task of generative leaders is to provide all relevant actors with a seat at the table where strategic issues are framed and strategic decisions are made, and actually activate them to take a seat. In the promotion of city development, which is a struggle between visions, development ideas and interests, those actors who are able to draw the attention of other actors and frame their thinking are influential. The combination of interpretive and network power seems to be a way in which to mould the preferences of the other actors. Neither interpretive power nor network power appear overnight: gaining them is a long process. It requires personal interaction with key people locally, regionally, nationally and often also internationally, and it also requires the conscious building of trust. Genuine trust and reciprocity are the core factors in long-term collaboration (Innes and Booher 2000). Furthermore, Innes and Booher (2000) argue that if the preconditions for trust are in place, the actors need no prior knowledge of each other to cooperate. Generative leaders aim to create these conditions and to connect people with the substantive knowledge and expertise important for the city, and this is the way they believe they can boost city development.

In the interviews, the Finnish generative leaders, both actual and aspirational, talked intensively about mind-sets, thinking patterns, perceptions, information, knowledge creation and other issues that are related to interpretive power. Even though interpretive and network power emerged here as more important than resource and institutional power, the importance of the latter should not be undermined. This is because the observations presented here are drawn from a study that focused on those local and regional development champions, many of them labelled as generative leaders, who, in spite of their assignment, did not have abundant resources or a powerful enough formal position in a governance structure to draw upon. Therefore, their approach is to influence legitimate power holders of the entire local/regional development system, local government, the corporate world and/or academia. They were working to create a new context and interpretation for the economic development of their respective cities and regions, and hence "to build a new storyline for a development play", as one of the interviewees put it, which therefore supports the importance of Lukes' third view and Foucauldian ideas of power being everywhere. All this also stresses the need to keep abreast of activities and developments in order to draw attention and raise strategic awareness.

> When one has learnt a new vocabulary and way of seeing things, it is easy to communicate everywhere and to interact with people, our way of doing and our way of talking being a bit different, it is easy to draw attention.
> (Development manager in a Finnish city government)

Generative leaders need to recognise dominant discourses and especially the dominant interpretations guiding the promotion of local and regional development, and to launch a new dialogue that might lead to a new hegemonic discourse on much needed changes and measures in the city. Leading by interpretation is crucial, because actors need shared beliefs to make sense of the ambiguous world and complex networks. Therefore, generative leaders aim to seek out both the differences and similarities in the various actors' interpretations, acting in order to synthesise different interpretations and the goals derived from them. They also aim to change and/or unify actors' interpretations of the city, its institutions, influence networks and so on (see also Klijn and Teisman, 1997). In practice, generative leaders convene groups of actors for dialogue, they mediate information and they also create new knowledge; they interpret, for example, academic thinking and talk to firms, and vice versa. All this both requires interpretive power and builds it. For these efforts leaders need to be able to speak with many interest groups in their "own language" not to alienate themselves from the relevant networks by speaking a language the rest of the pack does not understand or by using a rationale that has no meaning to people.

Interpretive power is fairly invisible by nature. It does not refer to efforts to seek consensus, but to an attempt to create fertile soil for shared thinking and joint efforts to transform the institutions for the future. The power to frame the issues discussed, to lead sense-making processes and hence to influence what issues are on the agenda and what are not, and hence also who is involved in the communication roundabout, brings a significant amount of power to an actor who can actually do all of this. As one of the interviewees, a development director in a city government, put it: "If you really want to influence, you must talk and talk, at least for two years. It takes two years to push a new idea through this community, and people then start realising what the situation is and what should be done and they want to participate".

The generative leader's key activities include also improving the coordination between fragmented groups of actors, fostering and organising collaboration and influencing, if possible, the division of labour within the influence network. In the influence networks, the different aims and strategies of many actors are continuously reconciled, various interests are balanced, and the touching points and the concrete means of making connections between many objectives are constantly looked for and coordinated. In this endeavour, we consciously use such terms as "to reconcile", "to balance" and "to coordinate" (Sotarauta and Linnamaa, 1998; Linnamaa, 2004), as it is doubtful that it is possible to base strategic action in influence networks on a shared vision and a shared will if reciprocal interests are not taken into account. A generative leader can influence by framing and enhancing the conditions for favourable, productive interaction among network participants. In aiming to coordinate the network or to integrate some parts of it more tightly together, generative leaders basically have three general options for achieving their purpose. First, they may take pains to create or shape institutions and structures (see Sotarauta and Pulkkinen, 2011), and hence generative leaders can frame development policies and processes and provide a context for the various networks and development activities. Influencing through the institutional set-up represents an aim to increase continuity in a rapidly changing world and provide actors with a clear and supportive playground. One aspect of coordination through institutions is to identify and demolish frozen shapes and hence to remove lock-ins. "Frozen shape" refers to configurations of administrative structures, government processes and thinking patterns which are static and not able to change to fit the changing environment, and thus they do not support development work. In practice, frozen shapes (i.e. old structures, mental models and institutions) are usually the worst enemies of effective networking.

> Of course, one part of this work is to strengthen competences, research stuff and suchlike, and in firms too, and we are especially happy if we can help in changing and building enduring structures, enduring structures for all that.
>
> (A leader from a local technology centre)

Second, generative leaders aim to coordinate by forging trust, mutual dependency, loyalty, solidarity and horizontal cooperation based on reciprocal support among organisations and individuals. This requires abilities in maintaining and deepening the sense of mutual benefit that exists within the network by enhancing network connectivity, integration (mutual adaptation) and transparency.

> My job is also to try to reduce mistrust, and build trust by my own actions; in this kind of network the process is never finished, situations change all the time. Our task is to interpret the conversations, and act as some kind of interpreters between different parties, and to try to prevent in advance difficulties from arising in communication and interaction relations. Better interaction, better forums for communication, that's our aim.
>
> (A coordinator of a university network for regional development)

Third, generative leaders coordinate by producing shared and often tacit knowledge. This leads to the social integration of actors, which extends far beyond the institutions themselves and the network, thus the ability to network competently and efficiently in order to utilise informal relations is of significant importance. The ability to share feelings, emotions, experiences and mental models becomes important (see Nonaka and Konno, 1998). Generative leaders need to find a way to blend the various participants – each with conflicting goals or different perceptions or dissimilar values – to fulfil the strategic purpose of the network. The leader seeks to achieve cooperation between actors while preventing, minimising or removing blockages to cooperation. This steering of network processes is tantamount to generative leadership in the sense that the result of the network process "derives from the interaction between the strategies of all actors involved" (Klijn and Teisman, 1997: 99).

Notes

1   This study comprised four main phases. The first phase was a literature review of leadership and power in local and regional development. In the second phase, 41 local and regional development officers were interviewed. In the third phase, an Internet survey was carried out with 531 respondents drawn from regional councils (21.3%), employment and economic development centres (10.0 %), technology centres and centres of expertise programmes (13.0%), local development agencies and local government (48.2%), and national level agencies and ministries (5.3%), as well as other non-classified actors (2.3%)

2   $((v1+v2+vn)/n)*20$.

6 Generative leadership as a relay in time

As previous chapters have made evident, an individual generative leader is not usually in a position to influence the course of events directly. As has also become evident, generative leadership is an interdependent and reciprocal process, a combination of strategic, interpretive, institutional and network leadership, focusing on giving birth to something new and especially on creating conditions for the stimulation of innovation in knowledge cities. Generative leadership is about searching for future directions for knowledge city development, bringing relevant actors together and constructing new thinking patterns. It is not a specialised role but a diffuse force that works over time, embedded not only in the respective governance system but also in a specific social and evolutionary setting. Generative leadership is inspired by transformational leadership that reminds us that in its attempts to bring about change, leadership has to (a) respect the identities of the many actors in a city, (b) act as a role model and inspiration to other actors and make them interested in issues related to the knowledge city development, (c) challenge other actors to take ownership of some aspects of knowledge-city development, and (d) understand the strengths and weaknesses of not only the city they work for but also the people living in it (applying Bass, 1991; Bass and Riggio, 2006).

It is argued in this Chapter that we need to move beyond relational but static conceptualisations and view generative leadership from temporal perspective. Therefore, generative leadership is seen as a relay process over time that is embedded in wider evolutionary processes. In a leadership relay, actors are engaged in a task or activity for a fixed period of time and are then replaced by other actors. A leadership relay for city development differs significantly from, say, a relay race. In a relay race, there is a fixed team and everybody knows their place in the team and the order in which one runner replaces another. Even more importantly, they know that they are members of the team and that they are participating in a race. In a generative leadership relay, it is much harder to know the team, coalition or organisation of which one is a member, and it may be as hard to know the meaning of the race and to detect its beginning and end. Additionally, the kind of relay discussed here usually has many "runners" on the track simultaneously; there is no clear order of runners and there are many managers, team leaders, anchor runners and other specialists "who all know best" the city's needs, and they both collaborate and compete with each other. Leadership relay is not a conscious, smooth and pre-designed process but rather a phase-by-phase process, an evolving search for next steps and visions. It requires different competencies and powers in different phases. The process is a contemporary version of "muddling through policies" (Lindblom, 1959), in which vision, strategy, network and sources of power evolve with situations.

In a leadership relay, leaders need to lead and work effectively within a constantly changing policy environment reminding that leadership is the art of asking the questions without the certainty of either a clear answer or the knowledge of who to ask or where to obtain correct answers (Trickett and Lee, 2010). For these reasons, the leadership relay is a never-ending process of influence, but is also a learning process taking place over time. It is prone to be broken by the many socio-economic and political incidents and interests, as well as by sudden and emergent environmental factors. Emergent forces and the intentions of individual actors may override the causal generalisations of the leaders and people may simply decide to do things differently (Dryzeck, 1993). As Dryzeck (1993) reminds us, interventions aimed at the course of development cannot be empirically verified without the intervention being realised; hence, the storyline guiding the development efforts needs to be stronger than the uncertainty caused by the lack of empirical evidence.

There is support in the literature for approaching generative leadership as a long relay instead of a static leader–follower relationship. MacNeill and Steiner (2010) observe that the leadership of cluster policy in Styria (Austria) was a continuous process of strategic development characterised by trial and error, rather than a linear process of strategy design and implementation. They also support the relational view by demonstrating the participatory nature of a strategy process. One of the key issues in their approach was to translate the theoretical concepts that had guided policy formulation so that they could be understood and accepted by wider networks of actors. Norman (2013) highlights the long-term nature of leadership, reminding us that if leadership lasts only a few years and is not able to renew itself, a power vacuum may emerge and that may again increase the fragmentation and complexity of the governance system. He (2013: 34) further says: "Lack of regional leadership usually implies that actors and institutions would use more time on coordinating, planning, and competing than they would if they could work in accordance with a regional leadership."

6.1 The main phases of generative leadership relay

The view behind the generative leadership relay is that bringing about knowledge city development and related institutional changes is a slow process that takes place over time. This view subscribes to Streeck and Thelen's (2005) argument that gradual transformation provides both academic studies and leadership with the most promising avenue for understanding and enhancing change in modern capitalist societies, instead of abrupt changes leading to discontinuity (breakdown and replacement). Streeck and Thelen's argument is in line with Campbell's (2009) conclusion that even changes that appear to be dramatic and radical are in practice less revolutionary than they may seem. Gradual transformation or "creeping change" denies the possibility of an optimum state and highlights constant search as the core in any institutional (organisational) change process. Hence, a punctuated equilibrium kind of change, where radical innovations take place between institutional reproductions, is not a viable option for studying change (Streeck and Thelen, 2005). This ontological argument is crucial. Since the optimum cannot be reached there always is a gap between the "ideal" and the "real" (Streeck and Thelen 2005). This argument reminds us that not all incremental changes are reactive and adaptive for the protection of institutional continuity. This view is realistic in the sense that generative leaders are seldom in a position to push for abrupt changes, but they may be capable of launching and directing "creeping change" that may ultimately lead to radical outcomes in the future, if successful. In this view, change happens as a result of an accumulation over longer periods of time of subtle, seemingly minor changes with a considerable discontinuity beneath the apparent stability on the surface.

Various studies related to knowledge cities (and regional innovation systems) often focus on ideas of system building and/or system repairing without a proper understanding that building and changing systems is a creeping and hence uncertain and creative process (Benneworth, 2007). Benneworth (2007) maintains that in cities and regions the issue is how they can change their collective developmental belief into something that can produce long-term prosperity in the place in question. In a way, he emphasises actors with interpretive power and Luke's third view on power. He adjusts van de Ven *et al.*'s (1999) notions on an innovation journey to the regional context. Benneworth's metaphor of the journey is here translated into the urban development game that was introduced in the opening chapter. Development games involve creating a new local vision during the play and experimenting with how it could be delivered. In addition, the game calls for shared understanding locally over the delivery of change. During the game, ideally, increasing numbers of stakeholders will join the players who initiated it, and as the number of players increase, there is a need to work to resolve the issues, tensions, vested interests and conflicts that such a deep-seated and fundamental game involves (Benneworth 2007). As the game evolves, players may feel that there are other games they want to play, or the game may change to something else, or it may come to a halt prematurely. There are always many issues creating pressures, which may lead players to abandon the game, and if there are not enough competent players, there is no game either. By definition, it is more or less impossible to lead multi-actor local development games with linear models or with one vision only, as it quite often takes time to understand what games the players are actually willing to play, and why they might be willing to join them. Development games are constrained by a sense of what is possible and what is not, as well as by legacies and foreboding. As Kay (2006) reminds us, this kind of process usually involves a series of interrelated decisions and actions that are shaped by earlier decisions and environmental factors.

The nature of a development game, as an uncertain and ambiguous set of sub-games, is exactly why we highlight the need to study the knowledge city development by adopting an actor-centric view with a leadership relay. For these kinds of purposes, Benneworth's (2007) schematised ideal-type process is the source of inspiration here (see also van de Ven *et al.*, 1999). It does not incorporate the uncertainty and ambiguity embedded in a game, but does offer a point of departure to work with. The view on leadership relay is adjusted drawing upon Sotarauta and Mustikkamäki's (2015), Drori and Landau's (2011) and Ritvala and Kleyman's (2012) empirical studies. It consists of five main phases: sowing the seeds of change, mobilisation, collective belief formation, the launch of activity and institutionalisation (Figure 6.1). These are by no means clear-cut phases; they intertwine in many ways. Leaders mobilise actors throughout relays, and the entire relay is about institutionalisation, as that is the only way to achieve sustainable outcomes. Additionally, instead of one grand game it is more likely that a city will progress along several independent or intertwined games that may be aligned or conflicting. One of the main challenges of any generative leader is to make them more aligned than conflicting. For the sake of simplicity, the main phases of leadership relays (a) are discussed as they were distinctive phases, and (b) sowing the seeds and mobilisation as well as launch of activity and institutionalisation are discussed in conjunction. A leadership relay often has these generic phases, which, of course, have different manifestations in different places and times. The generalised temporal schematisation helps us to study and understand the games and related leadership relays.

6.1.1 Sowing the seeds of change and mobilisation

The decision to begin a game is quite naturally often seen as the first step; a group of actors come together to express dissatisfaction with the non-desired developments, low levels of innovation, low renewal capacity, lost opportunities, etc., and a will to work collectively over public/private divides to address the identified problem (Benneworth, 2007). However, it may be difficult to detect how and when the first step was taken, and who initiated it. Often, the first visible step, the decision

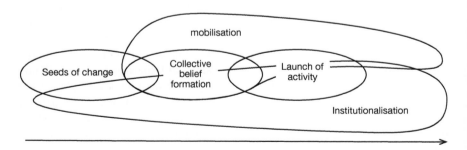

Figure 6.1 Idealised illustration of the main phases in a generative leadership relay

to play the game, creeps into many deliberations and policy discussions, and before surfacing and becoming visible it may have been simmering in the many influence networks for some time. The first formal and visible step may have been preceded by a more general discussion on the position of the city in the context of overall economic development, which plants (either consciously or unconsciously) seeds for later development (Sotarauta and Mustikkamäki, 2015; Sotarauta, 2014). It may even be that there is no explicit decision to come together, but merely that a small group of people feel that something must be done and that steps need to be taken, or that a broad societal discussion is taking place in the media that forces the leaders to react. Often this kind of small group worry or pressure from the media may lead nowhere, but if conditions are right, and leadership relays run smoothly, something major may happen. It may take a couple of years for a strategic influence network, not to mention a wider local community, to understand the actual situation and strategic challenges it is facing. Indeed, in the early phases of a specific development game, the leadership relay is inundated with uncertainty and leading figures are required to have both an appetite for risk and to be risk-aware, and/or to be passionate about their cause.

So, the launch of the actual development game is preceded by a phase that is here labelled "sowing the seeds". This refers to scattering such seeds, which are a source for future growth and change, over the local landscape, or detecting existing seeds and discussing and making sense of their meanings. If sowed consciously, seeds are scattered to do something that will cause a particular and wished for result in the future. Seeds may also be sown unconsciously by almost anything; a major economic crisis, new innovations and a change in the political scene are the most obvious sources of unconsciously planted seeds. Fairly often, those actors who sow the seeds for change may not know where they might all lead, but they may feel that something must be done and they simply want to awaken other actors and see what might happen. In any event, the most skilful of the generative leaders are capable of sowing seeds by themselves, identifying the potential for change in everyday matters or seeds planted by the other actors, and finding opportunities in externally caused crises. They also are capable of identifying external influences or seeds planted by others and building on these. In this phase generative leadership with interpretive and network power is usually called for, as resources and decisions on institutions and money will follow, but only if the relay is not broken before that.

Mobilisation starts with the identification of possible participants and stakeholders relevant to the issue in hand, and continues with the pooling of their skills, powers, knowledge, and resources. Potential participants have to be willing to devote resources to the influence network, and they also have to allow themselves to be influenced by actors who may have other interests at stake. It is not at all self-evident that firms, universities and other relevant actors want to become members of the various partnerships for knowledge-based city development. More often than not, they are not terribly interested in these kinds of collective activities. In Finland, local government often takes the lead in mobilising the various actors and creating new partnerships.

City government has a role to play here, or the public sector in general; they can promote these things (innovation systems and knowledge diffusion); they can be pretty good catalysts. Think of the Centre of the Expertise Programme, for example; it has been a good catalyst, and still is.

(Representative of a firm)

There are situations in which public interventions make sense; sometimes it may be a decisive factor that gets the whole thing going. So, you must respect their [firms and municipalities] competencies, the delicacy of their goals and suchlike; you just feed them with ideas, very gently, and hope that they will get interested in them and join us in promoting this and that. That is what we can do.

(A representative of one of the local Centres of Expertise)

Mobilisation is a very fragile and subtle process. Our interview data indicates that without a major crisis mobilisation is not a simple task and generative leaders actually need often to induce, or rather "seduce", various individuals and organisations to make them engage in the collective efforts and to maintain that engagement and commitment. Generative leaders cannot control and command other actors, and therefore a delicate understanding of the other actors' needs, strategies, visions, and language and thinking patterns are needed to get their commitment to the collective action; in the development games, "seductive moves" are needed instead of forcing moves. "Seductive moves" refers to such initiatives that other actors are not compelled to answer but actually want to answer, as these moves take into consideration the strategies and objectives of other players. If "forcing moves" are used to make another player yield to the will of the one who makes the move, "seductive moves" are used to try to make other players cooperate from their own standpoints.

I like the idea of seductive moves, it's a good concept. The whole style of communication is like a chameleon, you need different styles to communicate to reach different actors. That is one thing to recognise. Intuition does not help much here, you need to learn it; I mean what goes down with what group. One likes well-documented and argued proposals, one needs an enticing core idea, and you need to talk to some privately in the sauna. So, yes, there are many ways.

(A business development director in a Finnish city government)

It all starts by offering good openings, good opportunities to people; good from their point of view, I mean. They must find something for themselves, for their personal ambitions, an opportunity to learn something new, to gain visibility or to take a next step in their own careers, something like that . . . Who would not like to be a part of something big and important? We just need to paint a picture, create an image, and offer them roles in this puzzle to engage them in it.

(A business development director in a Finnish city government)

If actors have a seat, they also need a voice. All too often, actors are invited to participate in collective efforts for city development to legitimise decisions made, or to increase the credibility of forthcoming decisions without actually having real opportunities to shape the outcome of strategic decisions and direct strategic actions. In principle, all interests should be included in network processes (Innes and Booher, 2000), but, in practice, resources such as money, information and expertise are the integrating mechanisms of networks, and many actors without visible resources may become excluded – influence networks are asymmetric in nature, as power is not evenly distributed. Hence, it should be acknowledged that removal of network participants is one of the ways of leading networks and a central component influencing the dynamics of influence networks. Deactivation of actors quite naturally has potentially myriad effects on the network. The most common tactic in this regard is to introduce new actors as a means of changing the network dynamics and the power balance, and of shifting the influence of existing actors on each other (Klijn, 1996; Klijn and Teisman, 1997; Termeer and Koppenjan, 1997).

6.1.2 Collective belief formation

As pointed out in Chapter 1, a major challenge for leadership is to draw attention and then deflect it to the questions and issues that need to be faced (Heifetz, 2003), and as shown in Chapter 5, the highest form of power in leadership relays resides in the way in which actual discussions are constructed and in which problems and challenges are defined and framed, and how this is done. At this level, influence rests, as also argued above, on understanding the needs and resources of a whole series of different organisations with different objectives and strategies. Interpretive processes are central to framing the issues for action (Lester and Piore, 2004). Here generative leaders with strong interpretive power are called for, as other actors need to comprehend the purpose of adaptive or transformative measures so that they will focus less on the person and more on the meaning of the new action. Thus, various partners need to be actively involved in the belief-making process.

As also argued by Foucalt (1980), belief systems and collective construction of shared beliefs are often crucial, as the capacity of generative leaders to act as carriers of leadership relays depend on the dominant "social filters" and their ability to penetrate it. The social filter is a unique combination of innovative and conservative elements that favour or deter the development of a successful leadership relay, and most notably the capacity of generative leaders to mould social filters is important (Rodríguez-Pose, 1999). Social filters act as "conditions that render some courses of action easier than others" (Rodríguez-Pose and Crescenzi, 2008: 52). The social filter draws upon differences and similarities in actors' values, goals and perspectives on a given issue, and hence it is not just one social filter that needs to be penetrated to generate something new but several overlapping and potentially conflicting ones. "Belief" refers to probable knowledge, a kind of mental conviction and acceptance that something is true or actual (Webster's dictionary, 1996). Belief can draw upon many kinds of information and knowledge: religion, empirical studies, theories, experience, statistics and so on, and combinations of these. Ironically, if successful in their efforts to penetrate social filters, generative leaders often unknowingly work to construct new rigid social filters, potential sources of lock-in in the future.

Construction of collective beliefs to guide the wide networks of influence is based on enhanced strategic awareness. Awareness presupposes that actors know and recognise their own roles in the respective context. For the development of awareness it is necessary for a generative leader to aid the network in monitoring and interpreting events and making sense of them. Additionally, awareness expands to being strategic when an influence network has the ability to find the strategic issues essential to development from the long-term perspective. The main elements of strategic awareness are as follows:

- awareness of strategic intentions that are manifestations of an influence network – in practice, they are emerging processes about (a) the desired outcomes of the development efforts, (b) the position of the various actors in governance structures and (c) the establishment of the criteria to chart the progress (governance and strategy);
- awareness of traditions, past path and dominant trajectories, the changes in a city over time, i.e. the path that has been taken (history);
- awareness of the resource bases of a city (human, financial, physical and social resources) – possible opportunities and threats to them (resources);
- awareness of relevant knowledge – what is currently going on in research, industry and policy development in the fields important to a city (knowledge);
- awareness of the direction of present development, where we are going if the present development continues (trends);
- awareness of possible futures – both undesired and desired future alternatives (scenarios); and
- awareness of necessary changes and strategic issues (opportunities and threats).

The assumption then is that as strategic awareness grows so does the probability that policy-makers and other stakeholders will act in accordance with the designed strategies, and hence strategic plans may turn into pragmatic action, not so much on paper but in the collective awareness of the key actors. The gap between the intentions and the realisation of strategies may become narrower due to increased awareness. The basic methods of promoting awareness are seminars and workshops, the distribution of information through various channels, getting the media to cover relevant issues, providing successful examples, endless roundabouts of face-to-face discussion, commissioning studies on relevant issues, and so on. Strategic planning and foresight, according to our interviews, also play an important role in the collective learning of a new vocabulary and the penetration of existing social filters. From this point of view, strategic planning and foresight are not elements of rational policy-making but tools for constructing collective beliefs that orientate complex influence networks. Our interviewees talked a lot about raising strategic awareness. Without a sufficiently well-established awareness of the emerging issues and future prospects of a city, generating change is especially difficult, and generative leaders are not always able to penetrate the social filters, not to mention construct a collective belief on how to proceed. Raising awareness requires empirical evidence and almost endless discussion roundabouts with different interest groups and stakeholders.

> Awareness is an individual and grassroots-level phenomenon. General awareness of what happens and will happen in this city has improved a lot, and it will improve, but a hell of a lot work is needed to turn it into action – we agree on what the situation is like, but we do not agree on measures; that's where the fights are.
>
> (A development manager in a Finnish
> city government)

Strategic awareness is a necessary but not sufficient precondition for generative leadership. When strategic awareness is good, the opportunity for flexible and fast decision-making opens up. It is possible to decentralise the decision-making power to where things actually happen. If strategic awareness is bad, it becomes necessary to have possibly very fundamental strategic discussions over every single issue, which take time and may lead to a slow process due to the endless series of fires to be put out. It is exactly for these reasons why generative leaders aim to construct shared beliefs to guide collective action and thus also to mould social filters by using their personal networks and social skills in affecting others' cognition. Belief construction is a central part of generative leadership as leaders work, first, to see through a jungle of complementary and conflicting beliefs, second, to identify and acknowledge their own beliefs in relation to other actors' beliefs, and third, to construct a shared belief that allows collective development work. In doing so, generative leaders work to affect the ways actors construct their view of (a) what city development is like, (b) how knowledge of city development is acquired and justified, and (c) what it ought to be like (values) (applying Niiniluoto, 1989).

> If I think the core organisations here in this city, it's difficult to say . . . they should know, be aware of the situation, and that we must do something or we'll be in deep trouble . . . We can talk, and we do, but do we act on our rhetoric – it's not clear at all. Takes time, a lot of time.
>
> (A leader of a Finnish regional council)

To translate progress in collective thinking into collective action, strategic awareness needs to be framed towards a shared understanding of and vocabulary on the issues in hand. It is a prerequisite that collective action should be rooted in shared beliefs about required actions and the justifications for them. Belief formation is a process that is motivated by leaders' or an entire network's drive, interest and passion to use a versatile evidence base for change. Belief formation is dependent on knowledge justification, for which it is necessary to distill relevant knowledge from the cacophony of any urban development game. The justificatory process should not only be seen from the leader's point of view, since interaction with other players is required if new beliefs are to become part of the influence network's knowledge base and thinking. What comes to count as knowledge for a certain network is defined by its standards of justification, which are socially institutionalised in a given space and time (Sotarauta and Mustikkamäki, 2015, citing Yakhlef, 2010). Being usually quite well informed, generative leaders tend to forget that knowledge is not easily justified, social filters are not easily penetrated and strategic awareness grows slowly.

> Well, at first I wasn't even aware that they [various decision-makers in different organisations] were so ignorant about this [new innovation strategy for a city]. It was so simple and clear that I was under the impression that everybody knew about these things. Gradually I started to realise, because of the critique, that they were totally in the dark about this. They had no idea about the main clue here. I went to local councils, neighbouring municipalities and other organisations, and talked a lot.
>
> (A business development director in a Finnish city government)

Belief formation is used both during the mobilisation of the influence network and as a leadership process to find a direction for it, to influence the prevailing values and norms, and alter the perceptions of the network participants (Termeer and Koppenjan, 1997; Kickert *et al.*, 1997). Generative leaders can frame the network by introducing new ideas to the network and by providing network members with new interpretations of old ideas (Kickert *et al.*, 1997). Thereby, they aim to find common denominators both between individual goals and between individual and shared goals. The aim of belief formation is not only to find a shared perception of the issues in hand, but also to find a shared vision that goes beyond existing social filters and the shared vocabulary constructing them. Belief formation gives shape to emerging development needs and strategies, and hence also to collective efforts, and it has great influence on the alignment of various forms of engagement. The problem is that often our capabilities for recognising the open-ended exploratory parts of the development and innovation processes are not sufficiently well developed; we simply do not have a vocabulary for them; therefore, both interpretive power, strategic awareness raising and belief formation are constantly stressed here. They are among the stickiest glues in influence networks, even though they are difficult to achieve.

All that is said above argues that a truly shared vision can only emerge if such a strategic awareness can be generated that penetrates the existing social filter. This allows a collective belief to be formed, and that again is the basis for a shared vision (Figure 6.2). In this conceptual constellation a vision represents a desired future, collective belief refers to things actors collectively believe need to be focused

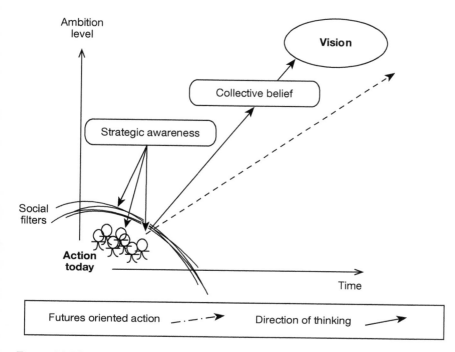

Figure 6.2 The conceptual relationship between social filter, strategic awareness, collective belief and vision

on and the reasons for doing so, and generic strategic awareness is needed for the penetration of existing social filters that lock entire governance systems and networks in the past. Strategic awareness is ideally based on a strong theoretical understanding and empirical evidence base, as well as on future-oriented thinking, while collective belief is more fundamental and sometimes may even emerge without any evidence base.

While the collective belief formation requires openness and disclosure, economic competition usually fosters opportunism, secrecy and sometimes suspicion (Lester and Piore, 2004). There also is a tendency in organisations engaged in influence networks to push interpretive processes to the margin and overemphasise power games, analytical problem-solving and short-term results. Interpretive power within influence networks is fragile, and the belief-formation process is easily disrupted. However, as Lester and Piore (2004) argue, economic development needs public spaces within which interpretive discussions can develop, spaces in which fears of the risk of the private appropriation of information do not disrupt the debate and collective framing efforts (Lester and Piore, 2004). These kinds of spaces do not easily emerge spontaneously, and hence, more often than not, this is what generative leaders aim to accomplish, combined with the need to construct collaborative spaces (see Chapter 3).

6.1.3 Launch of activity and institutionalisation

In the third phase of a development game, there usually is a need to demonstrate progress in the short term to keep the coalition moving on a selected path and to induce other players to join the game (Benneworth 2007). As Benneworth sees it, this is a prerequisite for more ambitious future activities. Indeed, progress is important in keeping the relay in motion. The players, individually and collectively, take measures to deliver projects that meet the identified needs (Benneworth, 2007). In practice, several measures are often taken before any game is launched, and it might be useful to see the third and fourth phase as focusing especially on the institutionalisation of new mental models, partnerships and structures for knowledge city development, and a leadership relay as carrying concrete actions and long-term structural changes. Conceptually, the launch of activity and institutionalisation are kept as distinctive phases of the leadership relay, acknowledging though that every measure, if seen from a long-term perspective, may be a step in a long process of institutionalisation. Institutionalisation is defined as a process whereby a new practice, activity, norm, belief or some other institution becomes an established part of an existing system, organisation or culture (Sotarauta and Mustikkamäki, 2015). Institutionalised practice has attained a high degree of resilience (Scott, 2001), and has become almost a rule in collective thought and social action (Mignerat and Rivard, 2012). Furthermore, d'Ovidio and Pradel (2013) add that the formation of collectives of actors who defend the emergence of a new institution is an essential part of the institutionalisation process.

So, all four phases of a generative leadership relay are about institutionalisation. The third and fourth phases are more visible than the first two and thus they are focused on in many studies. The argument here is that during the first two phases important work is done that is easily forgotten, and its relevance is not understood or not even seen. Therefore, these phases are focused on here more than the launch of activity and final institutionalisation.

6.2 Seinäjoki, Finland – from regional service centre of a rural region to regional centre of the knowledge economy

Seinäjoki is a small town in Western Finland (see Chapter 2). In this book it serves as an example of how small peripheral places may pursue knowledge city strategies. The case narrative follows the leadership relay sequence introduced above in its own way.

6.2.1 Seeds of change – collective anxiety and mobilisation of an influence network

The first step in the development game in Seinäjoki in the mid-1990s was not exactly a conscious collective step forward but rather a series of more or less well-integrated expressions of anxiety that "something must be done". At that time,

Finland was recovering from the fierce economic downturn of the early 1990s and research, development and innovation activities were heavily targeted nationally (Tervo 2005). Being located in the most rural of the Finnish regions, South Ostrobothnians were deeply concerned about their future prospects; the entire region and its centre seemed to be ill-suited to the emerging knowledge economy and related policies. Therefore, in addition to the economic challenges, the new rapidly changing Finnish regional and innovation policy landscape was both a source of anxiety and hope for South Ostrobothnia. As most of the local and regional development actors were trained and knew well the old subsidy-based regional policy, they felt uncomfortable with the new national policy that stressed endogenous efforts, the competitiveness of regions, technology and eventually also regional innovation capacity.

Being embedded in the collective anxiety, the development game started to revolve around an institutional core consisting of (a) the newly established Regional Council of South Ostrobothnia (the region) and (b) the Centre for Employment and Economic Development (the state), as well as (c) the Town of Seinäjoki (the local government). These three organisations are here labelled as the institutional core of local and regional economic development, as they all are assigned to promote economic development in the region. The leaders of these organisations clearly were assigned leaders. They aimed to exert influence through their own organisations, but they also aimed to reach beyond their formal assignments. The game was mobilised by these three institutional actors, individually as well as collectively. In spite of some tensions between the Town of Seinäjoki and the region (Linnamaa and Sotarauta 2000), the three institutional actors needed each other to push for institutional change. All of this was influenced by the Finnish multilevel regional development system that enabled and required the local and regional development agencies to regularly produce regional development plans and programmes, and hence raise local/regional development-related issues on the policy agenda. The formal multi-actor strategy design and implementation apparatus was in place, but it was not a sufficient condition for a truly collective strategy to be formulated.

The first steps on the game included analyses of the situation in Europe, Finland and South Ostrobothnia, which were extensively discussed in several planning processes, conferences and seminars, as well as in a regional development training programme commissioned by the Regional Council and organised by the University of Tampere. Virtually all the leading decision-makers and policy-makers, several representatives of firms and other key actors participated in the seminars and the training programme. Hence, they were given an opportunity to debate and discuss both the situation in the region and also the latest local/regional development theories; this took place not only among themselves but also with Finnish experts and authorities in the field. South Ostrobothnia and Seinäjoki are not among the most affluent places in Finland but are among the smallest and most rural. Consequently, the local/regional development organisations are fairly small and do not have the financial or human resources to produce results on their own, and thus they started to realise they needed each other to push for new paths.

The first phase revealed to the emerging strategic influence network how fragile the innovation capacity in Seinäjoki actually was, and how distinctively local and introverted the thinking had become. The key actors began to understand their own basic assumptions and deeply held beliefs about the development of the region and its centre and, most importantly, the limitations of these beliefs when faced with a new situation – the social filters began to quiver.

6.2.2 Collective belief formation – emergence of strategic awareness

Eventually, a collective strategic awareness began to emerge. At first, it ranged over the generic notion that something must be done, something that was not related directly to the traditional South Ostrobothnian targets for local/regional development such as village activity, agriculture, SMEs, machinery and the metal industry; instead, it was realised that new strategies ought to focus on something that would take into account, more generally, ways of strengthening the renewal capacity of the region and its firms as a whole. Innovation and academic research started to creep into policy-related discussions much more than was previously the case. This was a dramatic change in a region where academic research had traditionally been seen as a sign of hesitation and thus failure, and where university education had been considered to spoil a good hand.

In the late 1990s, the main strategy to strengthen the institutional capacity for innovation began to emerge and three interrelated schemes began to dominate the policy discourse. They were (a) the establishment of a science park in Seinäjoki, (b) the establishment of the Seinäjoki Polytechnic as the only locally owned higher education institute in the region (representing a merger between several colleges) and (c) the establishment of a university network to compensate for the thin organisational set-up for knowledge production and its utilisation (Sotarauta and Kosonen, 2004). In this chapter, the focus is on the processes, focused influence network and leadership that made the university network possible. It is fairly difficult to assess by whom, when and how the three main lines of action were established as they began to creep into deliberations, policy discussions, seminars, newspaper articles and so on step by step over the course of four or five years, and thus they also started to find their way into several planning documents. In spite of the emergence of strategic awareness and a collective strategy, which was beginning to take a visible, understandable and debatable shape, the concrete measures for how to proceed remained undefined for some time, as the collective belief in how to move forward was still to emerge.

In the late 1990s, three incidents gave a significant push forward, which on the one hand publicly challenged the thick social filters, and on the other hand provided concrete models with which to work. First, in 1998 the idea of establishing a university network received a boost from the Development Programme for Research in South Ostrobothnia in which the founding of a university network was officially presented for the first time as a concrete means of strengthening the quantity and quality of research in South Ostrobothnia, and of opening up channels to new knowledge created elsewhere. As the region did not have a long academic tradition, a conscious decision to focus on applied research was made. The programme provided the key actors with a legitimate platform on which to continue the search for the operational model for the network instead of the very generic ambitions and wishes that often lacked realism. Second, a group of fairly young academics from the local university filial units and the University Association took a lead in thinking about what a university network could actually mean in practice. They did not have a formal assignment to do so but, in practice, they initiated the collective belief formation process. As Sotarauta and Kosonen (2004) observe, the hidden aim of the group was to thrash out the matter of a university network and, if possible, to create an implementable concept for the network or to forget the entire idea. As the university network was not the only solution presented in the policy discourse, and as nobody seemed to know what it referred to in practice, the group felt it important to move on and clear the table. As the other initiatives focused on structural changes, the discussion tended to freeze as the initiatives would have been expensive to implement and more or less impossible to push through multiple chains of decision-making.

Third, in 1999, *Helsingin Sanomat*, the very same national leading newspaper that later praised Seinäjoki and the region, published an article entitled "Sunset Region" (Salmela, 1999; see Chapter 2). The article began by reminding readers that, after World War II, the South Ostrobothnian "farmers" believed that education spoils a good worker, and thus they did not establish a university in the region, even though they might have been able to do so. A professor from the University of Vaasa continued by maintaining that "the South Ostrobothnians are overly self-contained and self-sufficient . . . they will not co-operate with anybody if they are not forced to. And, the entrepreneurs are so old-fashioned that they are not hiring employees with a better education than they have received themselves, and what's that – primary school education?" The article irritated the South Ostrobothnians beyond imagination. In conjunction with some other critical publicity, the article boosted the development game.

6.2.3 Launch of activity and institutionalisation – a novel network of universities established

Gradually, toward the end of the 1990s, the analysis and strategic discussions in several workshops, revolving around the university network idea, resulted in an increased strategic awareness that the low quantity and quality of research was not of itself a problem. The conclusion was that the true issue for the town and wider region was that there were not enough competent individuals who could compete for national and international research funding, and who might be respected and credible actors in national and international circles (Sotarauta *et al.*, 1999). Consequently, the question of what might attract competent people to the region was raised, and the answer that emerged was professorships – the university network idea began to find its shape. In Finland, at that time, there were a more or less fixed number of professorships, and hence there was (and still is) usually fierce competition over these positions. The assumption was that there were plenty of hungry academics preparing themselves to compete for tenured professorships in their fields, and thus an opportunity to have a fixed term professorship in Seinäjoki on the "periphery of Finnish academia" for five years might later turn out to be a crucial factor in their career. An objective was set to found 12 new research professorships within six different universities (but located in Seinäjoki), and the professors themselves were supposed to attract funds for their own research groups (Sotarauta *et al.*, 1999). The network became known as "Epanet", and according to Riukulehto *et al.* (2009) the network and its acronym were not designed but born naturally from the social demand in the region. The natural emergence was significantly enhanced that the soil for it was prepared in several training programmes and planning processes that involved hundreds of people, and the collective belief formation was consciously lead. External to the region, the general feeling was of disbelief. It was not believed that South Ostrobothnians would be able to raise funding for 12 professors and that enough qualified researchers would apply for the positions (Sotarauta and Kosonen, 2004). But they were able to accomplish these ambitions.

As the Epanet network began to take shape and an endless series of negotiations began, it became obvious that the network could not continue as a free-flowing collaboration but it needed to be coordinated and managed. After further negotiations and new rounds of discussions, the University Association of South Ostrobothnia (established and funded by the municipalities in the region) was given the responsibility for the coordination of the Epanet network by universities and the three key institutional actors. The University Association, being a small independent association employing only a few people without big ambitions to develop Epanet to benefit itself, was seen as a neutral and objective organisation that everybody could trust (Rintala 2006). Universities were willing to work together but did not trust each other enough to let another university coordinate the network.

In the first phase of implementation (2001–2008), a network of six universities and 15 university professorships was established. The Epanet network generated unprecedented enthusiasm in the region; funding was raised for the professorships one by one. In 2009, in addition to the professors, there were 44 researchers and 41 doctoral students in the region on top of what was there previously. The research areas that were chosen represented disciplines that were believed to be important for the future of the region (broadly, these are regional development, welfare, food industry, production systems, and business administration). There was no basic funding from the government or any other single source; rather, the funding was a complex set of individual projects: (a) each professorship was a fixed-term 5-year project that was funded individually by those sponsors who saw the field in question as important; (b) the research and development projects the professors were leading were individually funded from international, national and regional funding sources (that all are competitive); and (c) the coordination of the Epanet network was a project mainly funded by the Regional Council of South Ostrobothnia and Town of Seinäjoki.

In 2001–2008, €9.4 million was raised to support the professors and their groups; altogether, they were funded by 96 private firms, 21 municipalities and 24 other public organisations. For the region, and its emerging innovation system, it was important that the professors, with their groups, were able to also attract international and national funding for their projects much better than had been the case in the region earlier. The combined revenue of all the research and development projects carried out by the professors and their groups in the period 2001–2008 accumulated a total of €20.4 million. Out of that, 52% came from national funding sources and 10% from international sources. The share of funding from regional firms was 17% and the combined share from municipalities was 19%. The network was able to meet the demands set for it: to become a nationally credible player and get firms more involved in the development efforts (Sotarauta *et al.*, 1999; Riukulehto *et al.*, 2009).

In the early years of the Epanet network, there was a conscious aim to construct a model that simultaneously served the needs of the national innovation system, local firms, regional development, universities and the individuals themselves. Serving a multitude of interests required a careful analysis of the interests of the network members themselves as well as of all the stakeholders. Stakeholder analysis was also one way of leading the coordination process, and it called for actors that were capable in exercising network power. What was proved to be especially important later was the decision to focus on nationally new, interdisciplinary and applied research subjects. The decision to specify the professorships so that they were nationally new in areas that were strong both in Finland and in South Ostrobothnia was a way to avoid direct competition with more established research concentrations. It was also a way to show that the question was not only about local/regional development but also about strengthening the innovation capacity of the entire country. Even though, from a national perspective, the numbers still are low in South Ostrobothnia, this kind of combination of national, regional and organisational rationales proved to be important in a situation where a few fairly powerful critics argued that the network was wasting research money in the interests of regional policy.

6.2.4 *The influence network and generative leadership in Seinäjoki*

The Seinäjoki case reminds us about the importance of the development system and the policy mix available for local and regional actors to exploit in their own collective strategy (see for policy mixes Flanagan *et al.*, 2011). However, the institutional arrangement is only a platform for seeking new collective strategies; it does not produce results without the actors having the capabilities to work together and push the collective strategy through to implementation.

In the early days of the new development game in Seinäjoki, institutional leaders with a clear assignment from the three core agencies had adequate institutional and network power and resources to bring actors together. The individual leaders of the local/regional development agencies had a good understanding of how the policy world functions in Finland, and thus they possessed the policy knowledge to launch the game and mobilise actors across the organisational boundaries. All of this was enabled by the fact that a severe economic recession in the early 1990s and Finland joining the European Union in 1995 penetrated the local social filters. The conclusion was clear – the future is not a direct follow-on from the past. At first, the institutional core was not able to move on with this realisation or translate the generic worries and anxieties into concrete strategies. Their substantive knowledge was not developed to a level that might have enabled them to more effectively lead the entire influence network; therefore, the network remained disintegrated and its discussions stayed at an abstract level, or focused only on very concrete short-term measures. They did not possess the substantive knowledge of innovation systems or the emerging regional development doctrine that was needed to construct a novel collective strategy and implementable solutions. In the first years of the game, reports and plans piled up. The three leading agencies lacked the vision and confidence to move from analyses and policy discussions to action. They were not able to construct such a collective belief in the region that would have pulled all the central actors behind a joint development strategy. For these reasons, development strategy was not crystallised and individual measure dissipated.

The early phase proved to be important for two reasons. First, as there was no actor with superior resources, power and/or knowledge capable of rising above the others, the sense of interdependency started to increase; this was a clear deviation from the earlier sectoral and independency-oriented thinking. Thus, a strategic influence network began to be formed. Second, extensive discussions and deliberations gradually generated a shared strategic awareness that was deeply rooted in the conviction that "we need to find a place in the knowledge/innovation economy – whatever it might be". At the outset, there clearly was a lack of knowledge about what "knowledge economy" or "innovation system" might mean. What proved to be crucial in framing the emerging collective belief was the willingness of the institutional core of the strategic influence network to open up the quite traditional planning processes of the very traditional region to fairly young academics who channelled new insights and possibilities as well as novel and substantive knowledge into the region. The institutional core tapped into the web of potentiality to expand the thinking in the region. New ideas, step by step, provided a community in collective anxiety with new insights to consider and concrete ideas to work on in the search for collective belief. The researchers were able to tell research-based and thus sufficiently convincing stories from other cities and regions of Finland as well as other countries. They were especially able to integrate otherwise separate theories and development models to meet South Ostrobothnian needs, and thus were instrumental in helping the influence network to tap into global networks for both explicit and tacit knowledge. Most importantly, they also were able to transfer and translate global knowledge into local language, thinking and action, and make interpretations about what all the innovation fuss might mean to the region. Additionally, at this stage, the influence network unlocked socially and historically embedded knowledge, and started to see more clearly than previously the kind of beliefs on which the earlier era of economic development was actually based.

However, even those actors who were intensively involved in the debates did not always fully grasp all the practical implications of the emerging strategy. Thus, to concretise the debates, the search for individual solutions to meet individual needs continued in the context of collective strategy making. One of the elements of success in the South Ostrobothnian development game was that collective and individual objectives were balanced, and while taking measures for the region or the town the actors were also able to strengthen their own position. This reminds us that influence networks and the leadership of them are not interest-free zones, but that a collective strategy orbits around individual interests. In the early phases, the public actors and academics led the process and the firm representatives, even though they were being actively engaged, did not take the lead. Later, after the Epanet model was constructed and individual professor projects started taking shape, the firms showed a willingness to take the lead in specific themes and projects that were designed under a shared strategy (Table 6.1).

6.3 Pitfalls of influence networks and a learning failure

The various difficulties that are faced in influence networks were not dealt with in Chapter Three, but it goes without saying that the strategic influence networks as well as more focused ones are not free of pitfalls. Case Seinäjoki reminds us that there are many kinds of interrelated pitfalls generative leaders are supposed to overcome and find solutions to (Linnamaa & Sotarauta, 2000).

In Seinäjoki, the institutional core aimed at constructing local and regional advantages through regional development plans, lobbying and also policy net-working. At first, most of the other organisations concentrated on their own interests and strategies, and did not actively seek memberships in wider strategic influence networks. The institutional core, consciously or not, aimed at directing the entire network but often the interdependence was experienced one way only. The other organisations participated in collective seminars, strategic planning processes and projects organised by the local/regional development organisations mainly to secure funding for their own projects or they felt it to be their obligation. They were present but did not necessarily contribute to the collective efforts. This kind of isolationist behaviour may lead to artificial influence networks that may end up being more a ritual based on the needs of the local/regional development administration or some other institutional power holders than actual collaborative work for the city or region. In these kinds of situations, collaboration may become an end in itself instead of focused and purposeful collective action. Isolationism may be due to, but not always is, shortage of collaborative forums. In Seinäjoki and more broadly in South Ostrobothnia, since the mid 1990's, there have been multitude of forums where all the key actors meet regularly to discuss both common and individual issues, and thus local/regional development organisations (in collaboration and independently) have worked to overcome the issue of isolationism and withholding of information. If key actors did not actively share information and generate new knowledge with one another, they would not under-stand each other's points of departure, logic, objectives and strategies, and thus

Table 6.1 The four forms of leadership by the main phases of the leadership relay and the development game in Seinäjoki

	Seeds of change, mobilisation	Belief formation	Action and institutionalisation
Institutional leadership	General anxiety is discussed and debated in the formal planning processes and training programmes.	General level national policy messages are transferred into the region but not translated into local belief systems.	International and national policy models are discussed and debated and their significance for South Ostrobothnia sought.
Interpretive leadership	Local/regional development organisations tap into web of potentiality to learn new theories of network-based local/regional development and innovation systems.	International and national experiences from the successful innovation systems are discussed and debated. The old convictions begin to crumble and new collective beliefs emerge.	A multitude of funding sources are combined to implement the strategy. Professors and their groups tap into sources of information that were previously unreachable to local actors. They transfer fresh knowledge to their partners and translate it to fit into the local situations.
Network leadership	No clear view on how the process ought to be organised beyond the formal planning process.	Some of the prevailing beliefs on how and by whom local development is led are unlocked, and new actors have a better seat at the table and stronger voice in the processes. Novel insights are translated to fit the local social fabric as well as the economic structure of the region.	Science, innovation, local economic development, regional and health policy knowledge are integrated to serve the local collective strategy. A complex myriad of actors as well as contracts and relationships of trust are coordinated. The University Association and the University Consortium of Seinäjoki coordinates and manages the network.
Strategic leadership	Distributed strategic leadership. Local/regional development organisations are each independently in the lead. Firms and local academics participate.	Local/regional development organisations lead the formal process. Academic community leads the thinking, firm representatives participate.	A new way of organising the relationship between knowledge production and its utilisation is constructed. Local/regional organisations enable the strategy to emerge. Private firms and universities lead the individual professorship projects.

also the needs of the place in question would remain in the dark. Lack of understanding of different ways of thinking economic development as well as the place seasoned with low respect towards different kinds of expertise was one of the most difficult of all the pitfalls to overcome in South Ostrobothnia.

So, successful leadership relay presupposes a sufficient number of forums to support the actors' opportunities for dialogue. This may also be of use in overcoming the most visible of all pitfalls that is incompatibility – organisations and the key individuals often simply do not get on together. However, it may also be that incompatibility is more of an outcome of the other causes than the root cause in itself, including shortage of spaces for dialogue, poor dissemination of information, ambiguous rules for collaboration, and fierce rivalry over scarce resources. Sometimes some of the influence network members lacking resources may cause tensions as they are seen as free riders who only participate to exploit other actors without any ambition to contribute to the collective development efforts. Influence networks require that each party be able to contribute some value added to the collective effort. It is also important to find proper roles for each network member, as unclear division of labour may lead to endless debates going round and round, freezing the development game in a never ending policy carrousel.

As network relations are based on trust and sharing of knowledge, the mother of all the network pitfalls is lack of trust. If trust is lost, time and energy are needed to restore it, and as the case Seinäjoki shows, collective construction of strategic awareness and shared beliefs through extensive informal dialogue and formal strategic planning is among the most efficient ways to build trust. Conversely, if trust is lost and knowledge not shared, an influence network usually falls in a situation that is characterised by lack of commitment that, for its part, leads to artificial and hollow networks. This again, may lead to lack of discipline. Influence networks usually have some "rules of the game" that are both formal and informal. If some of the actors do not respect these rules and primacy of partnership, they jeopardise relationships of trust. Too often leaders assume that actors commit themselves to the common good without seeking commitment from the perspective of actors' own points of departure and without accepting different ways of making a commitment. All the pitfalls briefly touched upon here are symptoms of a learning failure that refers to the situation in which actors belonging to an influence network cannot learn from their own and other actors' experiences nor incorporate anything new into their activities.

6.4 Leadership relay in a city – emergence of regenerative medicine in Tampere, Finland

To shed more light on the nature of the leadership relay, a study on the emergence of regenerative medicine in Tampere, Finland, is next used to illustrate how leadership relays unfold (for further information see Sotarauta and Mustikkamäki, 2012; 2015). This case differs significantly from the ones introduced in the previous chapter and in Chapter 3, as it focuses on a unique field of science and its societal and economic potential. It sheds light on a leadership relay in a city, as knowledge city development is always a tangle of more or less intertwined but independent change processes. Taken as a whole, they form the emergent entity that is here labelled as "knowledge city", without these kinds of individual leadership relays there would not be knowledge cities but only bold manifestos.

The term "regenerative medicine" was created in 2000 and is now widely used to describe biomedical approaches to healing the body by the stimulation of endogenous cells to repair damaged tissues, or the transplantation of cells or engineered tissues to replace diseased or injured ones (Riazi *et al.*, 2009). The Regea Institute for Regenerative Medicine is the reference point for this illustrative case. It was central to the emergence of the regenerative medicine concentration in Tampere, as well as becoming one of the cornerstones of local biomaterial concentration. Regea was established in 2005 as a joint institute of several organisations under the administration of the University of Tampere. It was established by the University of Tampere, Tampere University of Technology, Pirkanmaa Hospital District, Pirkanmaa University of Applied Sciences and Coxa, the Hospital for Joint Replacement. Regea's activities were based on three foundation stones: research, tissue bank operations and other services (e.g. renting clean room facilities, consulting etc.). The focal research areas are stem-cell research and research combining stem cells and biomaterials (Sotarauta and Mustikkamäki, 2015). In 2011, Regea was merged into Institute of Biosciences and Medical Technology (BMT).

The institutes themselves are only the tips of the iceberg in the wider story. Without plunging too deeply into the specifics of the science in question, the main outcome of the game is worth mentioning. In 2008, for the first time in the world, a patient's upper jaw was replaced with a bone transplant cultivated from stem cells isolated from the patient's own fatty tissue. The patient had lost roughly half of his upper jaw because of cancer. Since the treatment, the patient has been able to live a normal life with a normal upper jaw. In the process, the scientists were able to produce new bone cells by combining stem cells and biomaterials and then growing them into a jawbone of the correct shape and size (with the aid of a titanium frame) inside the patient's stomach muscle. In six months, the contents ossified and were filled with blood vessels and the designed bone and the surrounding muscle were then removed, together with the blood vessels, and fitted in place (Bionext, 2010). By the end of 2010, based on the technologies developed by Regea and then BMT and its collaborators, approximately 30 patients with serious bone deficiencies had been treated in Finnish hospitals (Bionext, 2010).

6.4.1 The seeds of change

This specific development game was launched by two professors from two different universities (the University of Tampere and Tampere University of Technology), who in the late 1990s clearly took the lead in pushing novel ideas forward and making new prospects visible. They did not have the institutional power required to take major steps forward by themselves, nor the knowledge of the policies and processes involved, but they were able to advocate the new potential of the local medical and biomaterial research, and hence they were able to launch the game and push it forward. At the same time, regenerative medicine had just started to progress rapidly at the global level, with tremendous hype as well as hope. The most positive commentators argued that regenerative medicine would become one of the three main forms of medical treatment, alongside medication and surgery (Valtakari *et al.*, 2007). The most negative commentators, for their part, argued that regenerative medicine consists of more empty promises and hype than actual treatment (for more, see Brown, 2003; Nadig, 2009). In Tampere, the key actors in the field of biomaterials started to realise the potential offered by research into stem-cells and tissue engineering, as did the local biomaterial firms. Importantly, the local science capacity in relation to stem cells and regenerative medicine in Tampere was fairly well established. Several research groups at the University of Tampere, the Tampere University of Technology and the Technical Research Centre of Finland (VTT) were involved in research on fat stem cells or biomeasuring (biological and physiological measurement of human beings) (Sotarauta and Mustikkamäki, 2015). At first, the local academic community was hesitant about exploring new opportunities. It saw the non-explicated ideas relating to new opportunities in stem-cell research and regenerative medicine as being too applied and fuzzy and, hence, outside their realm. Perhaps, by having a vested interest in maintaining their academic focus, they were not ready to give up their power base to search into unknown territories that might have changed their own position in the social fabric. As is well known, inefficient institutions often resist seeking fresh paths forward, because of the combined effect of social conflict and lack of commitment. In the case under scrutiny, the social filter was a thick one, preventing the emergence of a new path at that stage.

The first seeds of change were sown in this ground. The two professors who launched the process were non-assigned but both believed that there was "something more" to their research and more widely in their fields – something that, if applied correctly, might lead to new business, other forms of societal benefits, or would boost the competitiveness of existing biomaterial firms locally. This "scientific hunch" was founded on their expertise and long experience in their own fields. The two professors each introduced the idea of having an organisation for regenerative medicine in Tampere. The idea was fresh at that time. The professors were prevented from taking rapid action by two institutional obstacles: (a) the academic orientation of the University of Tampere, which focused more on academic excellence than the proactive search for new innovations or business ventures; and (b) the scarcity of funds and know-how for supporting innovation and commercialisation in this field (Sotarauta and Mustikkamäki, 2015). In retrospect, it is possible to see what the outcomes of the science in question have been, and the successful treatments provide us with a convincing story that there was indeed something in the air. At that time, nobody was able to explain exhaustively what the possible outcomes might be, and hence the first steps were hard to take.

6.4.2 Collective belief formation

The start of the relay hardly presented a novel situation for the advent of a science-based innovation. By definition, innovation challenges prevailing social filters and practices, and is often born in a climate of ambiguity, uncertainty and lack of clear vision (Lester and Piore, 2004). In this case, the initiators lacked the capacity to simplify the story and convince the institutional and resource power holders outside the scientific core of the future potential of the innovation. For these reasons, it is often difficult for policy-makers, funding bodies and possible beneficiaries to see the actual innovation through the hazy cloud of scientific reasoning seasoned with the general business noise generated by hype and hope, speculation and often fairly hollow innovation policy rhetoric more embedded in wishful thinking than factual evidence – a collective belief that does not have solid ground to put its roots into. On the one hand, formal institutions (the funding system, universities) as well as cognitive–cultural institutions were not immediately supportive. On the other hand, there was a local economic development system in place that proved crucial to keeping the process in motion. A local support community external to the academic spheres started to emerge to support the search by the two professors for new solutions to exploit the opportunities "in the air" (Sotarauta and Mustikkamäki, 2015).

The support community appears here to be a crucial factor in enabling the leadership relay to proceed without breaking. A support community is a group of actors who have a feeling of fellowship with others as a result of sharing common attitudes, interests and objectives in terms of their willingness to assist the process with all possible means at their disposal (see Sotarauta and Mustikkamäki, 2015). In this case, the support community consisted of local and regional economic development actors as well as interested experts from the universities and the Tampere University Hospital. The realisation of these kinds of ideas is at the core of the work of local development agencies, and many of them also shared the conviction of the professors that science is there for the improvement of society and ought to be commercialised if possible. Simultaneously with the intensifying local discussions, the tissue engineering industry (regenerative medicine) witnessed ever accelerating global growth (Lysaght and Reyes, 2001). This, of course, boosted the enthusiasm and belief in local capacity, and fairly quickly the support community decided to aim for a global business. The previous experience of one of the leading professors that this could actually be done and his status as a local role model in translating science into practice provided a strong impetus to the process.

The support community established a planning group that, in a way, decided to play the game. Hence, the second phase witnessed new actors taking the lead. The leadership relay moved beyond the academic sphere when the support community began constructing a collective belief and a financial base for exploiting the global potential and expanding local opportunities by strengthening local capacity and resources as well as searching for possible next steps. The first two phases were based on a conviction that there actually was a rapidly growing global market to be exploited, but it soon became obvious that the technology was not mature enough and true business opportunities were still too far away and over the horizon. Consequently, there was no business and hence no venture capital either; the entire field appeared risky and enthusiasm started to wane. Indeed, there was no demonstrable progress along a selected path. The local planning group realised that it was not possible to accomplish the business plan; there were no global business or local business competencies to push this rather unique field forward (Sotarauta and Heinonen, forthcoming). Even though the game was almost abandoned in this phase, the leadership relay was not broken, and it was able to carry forward the idea through the difficulties. The local potential was seen as too promising not to be developed further and the feeling of prospective progress prevailed and new paths were actively sought. The discussion moved onto emphasising both the basic and applied research – if there is no business opportunity, then the research capacity at the university should be strengthened by launching a major research project. This later resulted in the Research Institute for Regenerative Medicine, which became later a part of the BioMediTech. This phase also indicates that collective belief, to truly serve the leadership relay well, needs to be flexible. Actors need to change their most dearly held assumptions if new empirical evidence is presented – this is easier said than done.

6.4.3 Launch of activity

The game was not abandoned at the end of the second phase because the key actors were able to learn and reinterpret their beliefs and find new solutions. They reinterpreted their assumptions and thus moved from the constructed collective belief to action in which, as Benneworth (2007) maintains, the players individually and collectively take measures to deliver projects that meet the identified needs. Simultaneously, the support community started to change gradually. If, in the second phase, the leadership relay consisted of local and regional development agencies possessing interpretive and network power, now the research and clinical community with its institutional power and substantive knowledge took on a more prominent role. This also meant that interpretive and network power, so dominant in the construction of a collective belief, started to diminish and institutional and resource power began to be the main driver again. The leadership relay moved from the support community back to the academia, especially into the hands of the leadership of the university and the director of the newly established research institute.

The collective belief that was constructed in phase two proved to be sufficiently enticing to the requirements of a broader range of stakeholders of regenerative medicine. At this point, it was significantly easier for the resource holders and decision-makers to see what might lie ahead. Instead of establishing a business venture, the launch of the activity included three main actions: (a) the establishment of a tissue bank, (b) the eventual establishment of the Regea Institute for Regenerative Medicine and (c) the recruitment of person(s) to lead Regea. In a way, with the establishment of the institute and successful treatments, the last step of Benneworth's schema was witnessed. A satisfactory destination was reached.

The destination is reached when the main barriers to innovation have been addressed and the game ends with renewed institutions and/or new institutions (Benneworth, 2007). In practice, development games never end, and that has also been the case in Tampere. The institutional basis for regenerative medicine has been expanded by collaboration between the two universities, and after becoming properly institutionalised the emphasis is, again, on commercialisation – the game continues (Sotarauta and Heinonen, forthcoming).

As already indicated above, a leadership relay may come to a halt at any phase and several competing ideas and solutions can challenge it and the networks and actors involved. Market forces and the government, legislation, the media, competing influence networks and so forth provide tremendous challenges for development games and any individual policy solutions. This implies that there are policy windows in which certain ideas and policies are accepted while others are rejected (Kingdon, 1984). This may help us to understand why local development games so often fade away and fail to produce the desired results. Both the difficulties in putting the collective act together and emergent developments may stop the game or completely redirect it. The question is not about the simple, coherent and unique design and implementation of a strategy, but about a complex bundle of different policy logics and ideas that reach way beyond single policy domains into many economic, political and social spheres of life. And here, the mechanisms that underlie path dependency in the strategy process are a form of context-bound rationality among players in a game (see Table 6.2).

Table 6.2 Leadership by the main phases of the leadership relay and the development game in Tampere

	Seeds of change	Belief formation	Institutionalisation
Institutional leadership	Not involved.	The support community consisting of local and regional development agencies and some academic actors take the responsibility and lead the process and fund the planning.	A multitude of funding sources are combined to institutionalise regenerative medicine in Tampere. Science, innovation, local economic development, regional and health policy and funding knowledge are integrated to serve the collective strategy. University of Tampere takes the lead in institutionalisation.
Interpretive leadership	Scientific hunch leads the way but no clear view on how to move forward.	International developments are analysed, data are collected and the future prospects of regenerative medicine in Tampere are discussed and debated. Some of the prevailing convictions about the role of the science in question are challenged and structural holes in the local institutional fabric are detected. A new collective belief emerges, which proves to be based on wrong assumptions and knowledge, and is to some extent reconstructed.	The collective belief constructed and reconstructed in the previous phase guides the institutionalisation process. The directors (each in their turn) of the related institutes at UTA lead the thinking.
Network leadership	The two professors tap into the local strategic influence network and thus reach beyond academia to seek help from the local and regional development agencies.	Relevant local actors are integrated in the focused influence network to search and plan how to exploit and strengthen the local innovation capacity.	A wide spectrum of local, regional and national actors are involved. International web of potentiality is explored.
Strategic leadership	No real strategic leadership.	Local/regional development organisations show the way.	University of Tampere in collaboration with the Tampere University of Technology in the lead. National funding bodies enable the institutionalisation.

7 Generative strategy

7.1 Why strategy?

As discussed in Chapter 2, the common strategies for constructing successful knowledge cities focus on enhancing the research excellence of universities and other higher education institutions as well as R&D organisations by attracting both knowledge-intensive firms and creative and innovative individuals to the city-region, using many channels to brand a city as a knowledge city, enhancing the quality of place, securing fast transport connections and advanced communication networks, and working towards developing the international and multicultural character of the city – and all this is dependent on specific leadership relays aiming to accomplish specific objectives that again calls for political and societal will, strategic vision and dynamic long-term strategic planning, agencies that are dedicated to the promotion of knowledge city-related processes, strong financial support, partnership and strategic investments, and value creation for citizens that comprises skill development, employment and social outcomes (Carrillo, 2006; Landry, 2006; Yigitcanlar *et al.*, 2007; Carrillo *et al.*, 2014). Knowledge city strategies may focus on many things, and it is quite often stressed that these development efforts ought to be comprehensive in nature. It also is believed that the effective and collective promotion of city development requires influence networks capable of articulating visions of different futures, and also of trans-forming "blue-sky thinking" into focused strategies and collective action. Existing social filters ought to be penetrated and shared beliefs constructed to guide the collective action, and this is attempted with the help of local and/or regional strategies and shared visions (Valdaliso and Wilson, 2015). In other words, it is hoped that city strategies and shared visions would not only guide city governments but also more broadly the influence networks with the maximum number of local/regional/national actors, either directly or indirectly.

However, governance structures and procedures are often too fragmented and competitive to enable instrumentally rational and comprehensive knowledge city strategies to be formulated and implemented. A shared vision-based strategic direction setting for the knowledge city seems to have its limits. It might be better not to chase the illusion of a shared vision and strategy but to search for alternative ways to work strategically to promote city development. The proposition here is that the collective strategic planning provides both individuals and collectives with an organised forum in which to create and maintain strategic awareness, construct collective beliefs and seek collaboration, but not always a shared vision and plan to implement them. Generative leadership may be one of the forces that sets development processes in motion and works to shepherd them towards their implementation. In this chapter, the aim is not to outline a comprehensive picture of strategy development in knowledge city development, which is beyond the scope of this book (for schools of thought on territorial strategy and the practice of strategy making, see Valdaliso and Wilson, 2015). Instead, this chapter elaborates the nature of strategy making from the perspective of generative leadership – what do we need strategy for? This issue is discussed using both theoretical insights and an Internet survey carried out among the participants of the Helsinki Metropolitan Area (HMA) innovation strategy process (Appendix 2), as well as among those key actors who did not participate. The survey[1] was to elicit information about the perceived uses and benefits of the strategic plan and the strategic planning process (for more detail, see Sotarauta and Saarivirta, 2012). Helsinki Metropolitan Area is a relatively complex and versatile metropolitan city-region that has a strong but fragmented local innovation system. Being the only metropolitan area in Finland, with its 1,485,000 population (in 2014, see PX-Web Statfin Database, Statistic Finland; for more, see Pelkonen, 2008) and having a very strong institutional and organisational basis for a knowledge economy, it dominates the Finnish innovation scene in many ways. The number of employees working in R&D is the highest and the educational level of the employees is similarly among the highest in the country. Knowledge generation and its application and the higher education sector are very important to the economic development of the Helsinki Metropolitan Area. There are several universities and polytechnics as well as research centres, and many dominant Finnish firms.

Strangely enough, for a long time the Helsinki Metropolitan Area remained fairly passive in local efforts to boost competitiveness and increase innovation capacity, while many of the other Finnish city-regions had aimed to achieve exactly these since the early 1980s (Linnamaa, 2002; Tervo, 2002; Männistö, 2002; Kostiainen and Sotarauta, 2003; Pelkonen, 2008). In a way, the key actors of the HMA only awakened in the 1990s to the realisation that even in Helsinki, which has a dominant position in Finland, there is a need for comprehensive and collaborative local economic development and innovation strategies (for a detailed analysis, see Pelkonen, 2008). This was a demanding realisation. One might argue that prior to this awakening the key policy actors of the HMA mixed the existence of nationally important knowledge creating and exploiting organisations with a strong local innovation strategy. Many of the key organisations were managing fine on their own (e.g. Nokia, universities, polytechnics, etc.), but to do well in the face of fierce global competition, as was argued and believed, the HMA needed an innovation strategy to create even better conditions for innovation. The idea was initiated in the so-called Helsinki Club II, which was summoned by the Mayor of the City of Helsinki. All the relevant stakeholders participated in the strategy making (altogether there were 115 participants, see Innovation Strategy, 2006).

7.2 The basic tenets of the classical approach to strategy and strategic intentions of the Helsinki Metropolitan Area

In spite of the huge amount of literature on strategy, there is no single, universally accepted definition of the concept. Different authors, planners and managers use it differently. Neither is there a single standard approach to strategic thinking, planning or management (Mintzberg, 2000), even if classical strategic planning dominates many spheres of policy-making.

Henry Mintzberg provides a very basic and widely used distinction between intended strategies and realised strategies. According to Mintzberg (2000), it is also possible to distinguish deliberate strategies, where intentions that existed previously are realised, from emergent strategies, where patterns are developed in the absence of intentions, or despite them. Strategies may go unrealised, while patterns may appear without precondition, as pointed out in Chapter 1. Based on these notions, it is possible to propose that in the Helsinki Metropolitan Area there were strong emergent local development strategies but collective intended strategies, not to mention deliberate strategies, were poorly developed before the efforts in the 2000s. Of course, for a local innovation strategy to become truly deliberate would seem to be unlikely. Precise collective strategic intentions would have had to be stated in advance by some kind of wider centre of influence network and then these would have had to be accepted by everyone else, and then realised with no interference from the market or from technological or political forces. Naturally, as Mintzberg (1992) maintains, a truly emergent strategy is also unlikely. It would require consistency in action without any hint of intention. In local innovation strategy, the question is about the interplay between intention and emergence. This is exactly why we treat generative leadership as a nexus between intention and emergence.

Whittington maintains that the intention-oriented classical approach is rooted in the idea of rational planning and its methods. For classicists, strategy is an essential part of shaping the future. The classical approach considers the possibility of having a monolithic goal of some kind as the natural outcome of strategic planning. Classical theorists see strategy essentially as intentional and deliberate (Whittington, 1993). The approach used in Finnish local and regional development is usually based on the classical approach. When strategic planning started to attract Finnish policy-makers in the early 1990s, the methods of the classical approach provided them with an appealingly ordered and clean view of strategy making (Linnapuomi, 1990; Sotarauta, 1996). It was sufficiently dissimilar but still similar enough to previous rational planning models to attract their attention. It is no wonder that public sector actors preferred the classical to the more modest, practical and perhaps too realistic processual view that often sees organisations and evolution as incoherent and muddled phenomena.

The five basic premises of the classical school identified by Mintzberg (2000) are used here to simplify the discussion on classical strategy. First, strategy formation is a controlled conscious process and therefore the action does not receive as much attention from the classicists as the reason for the action – action follows once the strategies have been formulated. The belief is that strategies come out of the design process fully developed, and they should be made explicit and articulated. Second, when unique and explicit strategies are formulated, they must be implemented (Mintzberg, 2000). Local and regional development discourse and practice is more often than not in line with these assumptions. In the rhetoric of city development, strategy usually refers to a consciously developed outcome that is presented in written form in a "city development plan/programme" or in a "local innovation strategy", and implementation is seen as a distinct phase in the strategic process.

The third assumption, according to Mintzberg (2000), is that the responsibility for the process must rest with the chief executive officer or a coalition of some kind: that actor is the strategist. This premise reflects both the individualism and the military notion of the solitary general at the top of the hierarchy. Strategies in this sense are strategic orders for the organisation to carry out. However, in the networked settings of city development this assumption is not viable. In fairly complex governance settings and with many influence networks working on knowledge city development it is not usually possible to identify "The Leader", and in the spirit of governance it is not possible to identify "The Organisation" that might alone have a leading role either. For these reasons, the aim is to create some kind of influence network to take responsibility for the core projects and processes of city development. It is important to notice that, in the context of influence networks, strategy is used differently from the corporate world. In the corporate world, strategy is widely seen as general-level "orders" to the organisation, while in the local development world, it should be seen as one of the tools to construct a collective inter-organisational development effort.

The fourth assumption states that the model of strategy formation must be kept simple and informal and the fifth one argues that strategies should be unique. The best strategies result from a process of creative design and are built on core competencies (Mintzberg, 2000). The HMA innovation strategy aims to be a classic strategic plan outlining the HMA position, the required development trajectories and the main actions. It contains bold ambitions as well as concrete measures. There are no data available to assess how well the HMA innovation strategy has been realised, but what is obvious is that the strategy and the vision presented in it are hardly unique constellations; many of the strategies in different city regions across Europe resemble it and each other.

> *The vision for Helsinki Region:* The Helsinki Metropolitan Area is a dynamic world-class centre for business and innovation. Its high-quality services, arts and science, creativity and adaptability promote the prosperity of its citizens and bring benefits to all of Finland. The Metropolitan Area is being developed as a unified region close to nature where it is good to live, learn, work and do business.
>
> (Innovation Strategy, 2006, p. 5)

The four pillars identified in the strategy document provide us with a generic overview and give a flavour of the collective endeavour. The strategic pillars are:

(i) improving the international appeal of research and expertise, (ii) reinforcing knowledge-based clusters and creating common development platforms, (iii) reform and innovations in public services, and (iv) support for innovative activities (Innovation Strategy, 2006). The four pillars are supported by twenty-six fairly concrete action proposals.

In the case of the HMA innovation strategy, 64.5% of the respondents of the survey perceived that participating in strategy making increased either very significantly or significantly their strategic awareness of the importance of local innovation systems, their main features and the participants' own roles in the development of the HMA innovation system. In addition, 71.9% perceived that the strategy process enhanced their strategic awareness of the position of the Helsinki Metropolitan Area in the global competition between cities. Additionally, 50.5% of them claimed that after the strategic planning process they understood better than before the links between global developments, a knowledge-based economy and the local efforts to boost innovativeness. The Internet survey also asked, in the spirit of classical approach, whether the HMA innovation strategy creates a "shared strategic intention and vision" among the key stakeholders. If strategy making had clearly affected the emergence of collective strategic awareness, it had not led to shared strategic intention yet. Only every fifth respondent (20.7%) saw that a shared intention had emerged due to strategy work, while 41.9% did not notice any such development at all. At the same time, a majority (63.9%) perceived that there was now a better-established shared vision among the key players. Additionally, 74.9% of the respondents believed that the most important targets of the development efforts had now been identified, 69.8% of them saw that the concrete measures to be taken had been identified and 62.3% saw that the strategy development had launched new collective development processes. Interestingly, the survey results suggest that strategy making increased strategic awareness, enabled the emergence of a shared vision and answered the question of what needs to be done next; however, all of this had not led to a shared strategic intention or a wider commitment to strategic operations.

Based on the Helsinki experience, it is possible to conclude that the making of an innovation strategy significantly increases the strategic awareness of those who participate and support the emergence of a collective belief. Therefore, it is also possible to conclude that strategic planning is a collective and organised mode of strategic thinking and one of the main ways to construct collaborative advantage through increased strategic awareness. Strategic planning is a collective way of making sense of a complex flow of events, and it may serve generative leadership well in its effort to penetrate social filters and construct new beliefs.

7.3 The black hole of classical strategy

In the promotion of economic development, many European city-regions have conformed to the core assumptions of classical strategic planning. In addition, in line with the literature on governance and networks, the principle of partnership has been used to stress that behind local strategies there are several organisations that should participate in the promotion of local development and formulation of collective strategies for that purpose. For example, Trickett and Lee (2010) call for cross-cutting leadership that is capable of developing and delivering a collective vision. Indeed, quite often the key qualities of effective place leadership are seen to be the formulation of a realistic vision – the achievement of a high level of approval and commitment to it and finally leading by example to realise it (Beer, 2014). Consequently, the classical strategy applied in the knowledge city context expects that (a) the strategy should be based on the shared vision and objectives of several organisations, (b) the strategy should guide activity of many organisations and people, and (c) strategic analysis concentrates primarily on the characteristics of the city-region while the characteristics, resources and competencies of the organisations and people carrying out the strategies are not paid adequate attention to.

As classical strategic planning does not fit in the modern governance settings and related influence networks as well as often imagined, the use of classical strategic planning in urban and regional development has not been free of problems. Experience has shown that a technically clean strategy document (a plan) is relatively easy to formulate, but that its implementation is rather difficult in its planned form (Sotarauta and Lakso, 2000). In many cases, the function of strategic planning has been to provide reassurance as much as guidance. Strategic planning provides breaks in the midst of operational functions by providing an opportunity to discuss the vision and other abstract issues. Many members of strategic influence networks have found that strategies incorporate many nice thoughts and principles, but they have had difficulties comprehending their real essence in terms of their own organisation or the city-region as a whole. They have difficulties combining abstract thinking with operational matters.

The simple articulation of a vision for a city is insufficient to establish leadership. Instead, while the articulation of vision may be a necessary phase in the leadership processes, leadership appears to be a much more complex and contested set of roles, and often its vision may not even become codified, finding its expression in a simple commitment to put the place first, regardless of opposition or wider concerns (Beer, 2014). The generative leadership relay demonstrates the different roles of strategy and vision from what the classical approach suggests. Vision indeed is an important element in leadership, but not as linearly as often thought. One of the basic problems is that while knowledge city and innovation strategies have been seen as plans, but in influence networks complexity easily replaces clarity and comprehensiveness replaces cohesiveness; or, as is often the case, strategic plans remain at too general a level and their power to guide the actions of many organisations is poor. For these reasons, among others, strategic planning is easily divorced from the process of implementation. In times of rapid change, it may be that the implementation gap cannot be reduced simply by formulating better strategies and committing ourselves better to them – we need leadership models that recognise the non-linear nature of leadership and thus also strategies.

More often than not, policy-makers have too strong a faith in classical strategic planning, and therefore there is always a danger of falling into the **classical**

strategic planning trap (Sotarauta, 1996), which is based on the too well-established a belief that (a) planning and implementation can be separated; (b) the quality of the strategic analyses guarantees the quality of the intended strategy; (c) the quality of the intended strategy's contents guarantees its implementation; (d) that it is possible to have various organisations fully committed to the local strategies already in the planning phase; and (d) that it is possible to distinguish on the one hand the strategic level that is responsible for the formulation of local strategies, and the operational level, which is responsible for implementation, on the other hand. The question is not about a trap de facto, but rather about not entrusting the planning for the future to classical strategic planning methods only. If they are overemphasised, the quality of the everyday process is easily neglected (i.e. the preconditions for learning, communication and trust). A Finnish local leader explains what makes the implementation of classical strategies become divorced from well-formulated collective intended strategies:

> Making choices is always difficult, and in a large networks it is even more so. There are always people who follow the golden rule that everything is important and in varying order on different days. In my opinion, they are benevolent fools who knowingly or unknowingly can't make choices . . . to take responsibility for futures.

For these reasons, many strategies are designed so broadly that visions and strategies are "nice and easy to support" because they exclude almost nothing. In Finland, many (not all) of the urban development strategies or shared visions do not mandate any radically new directions, but rather they confirm and strengthen the directions initiated earlier. Strategic planning provides networks with many good tools and thinking patterns, but quite often the designed strategies fade away and disappear into a "black hole of classical strategy development" (Figure 7.1) – visions are created and strategic objectives identified, but measures dissipate, and in the end, in the worst cases, strategies do not have any guiding effect.

> Our (local development) strategy is good on paper but how many of us work on it on a daily or weekly basis, may I ask . . . When we face tough situations and need to make hard decisions to keep following our strategy, we start losing people, not many are left in those situations. And then those emerge who want name the culprits, even before the actual failure. Not many are resilient enough to promote these things day after day, year after year.
>
> (Development manager of a Finnish city)

The black hole is caused by the fact that there are many objectives and endeavours in influence networks, not to mention the entire urban governance ensemble. Even the question "What is development?" may prove hard to answer. Moreover, such questions as "What are we aiming at?", "How are we acting together?" and "How are resources to be channelled?" may be very difficult to answer as each of the various actors contemplates development from its own

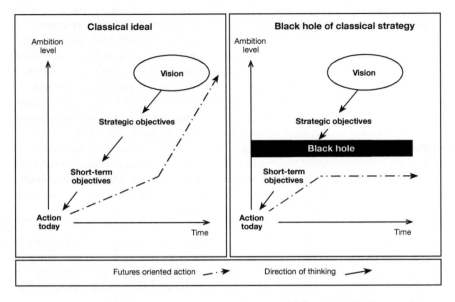

Figure 7.1 Simplified illustration of the ideal of classical strategy development and how the ideal vanishes into the black hole of classic strategy, and short-term objectives and action diverges from the vision

perspective. These are the reasons why collective belief formation was so strongly stressed in the previous chapter. Even though in many countries city governments play an important role in city development and many influence networks, they are in no position to direct or control the strategies of enterprises, organisations, families and so on. Often strategy preferences emerge from dynamic processes and are thus also dependent on the logic of the situation and political judgement about what is feasible and what is not. Thus, leadership relays and strategies as tools of generative leaders ought to be seen as iterative processes that are built around "real" economies and local understanding (Trickett and Lee, 2010). Collective action requires a form of leadership that generates, renews and sustains the collective learning cycle over extended periods of time. In these kinds of processes, leaders often lead without institutional power, and hence, as was shown in Chapter 5, interpretive and network power are important, and thus strategy making is one of the most important ways of exerting indirect influence. The process view and the four forms of power stress the need to understand strategy as an interface between different spatial scales, mixes of hopes and fears, and the intended and unintended consequences of any intervention. Generative leaders use the strategy process as a tool to manoeuvre through a riptide of strategic intensions and emergent forces. This observation takes us back to the issues related to the social filter, strategic awareness, collective belief formation and shared vision, and to the proposition that instead of seeing shared vision as one of the elements in strategic planning it might be useful to see it as a long process of social construction of collective beliefs taking place in leadership relays. All this, among other things, leads us to approach strategy as a process instead of as a planning procedure.

7.4 Processual approach in strategy – what roles for strategy?

As said, experience in many cities has shown that a strategy document (a plan) is relatively easy to formulate, but implementation in its planned form is rather difficult. This frustrates strategy makers, or at least it should. It may well be that the problem is not in the capabilities of strategy makers to design brilliant strategies but in the fact that classical strategic planning has promised too much to influence network dependent city development. For that reason, for some time now, there has been a move away from overly classical approaches towards a softer grip. As Morgan stated some time ago, the managers of the future will have to learn to ride turbulent conditions by going with the flow and recognising that they are always managing processes and flux, rather than stability defining the order of things (Morgan 1991). Morgan's future is today.

As has become obvious, hopefully, generative leadership is a temporally sensitive and process-oriented view that changes some of the dearly held assumptions of strategic planning too. In a way, generative leadership emerges, at least partly, from the criticism of the classical view on strategy in local and regional economic development and from the attempt to avoid the trap of classical strategic planning. It is aligned with a processual view of strategy, even though it accepts that classical strategic planning methods also have their place as parts of a process. For processualists, cities, organisations and markets are incoherent and muddled phenomena. Strategies emerge with much confusion from the incoherence and in small steps. The best that can be done is not to always strive after the unattainable ideal of instrumentally rational fluid action, but to accept and work with the world as it is. Here it is essential to abandon the idea of the instrumentally rational strategy designer. Mintzberg (1994) describes the basic idea of the processual approach interestingly: "real strategists get their hands dirty digging for ideas and real strategies are built from the occasional nuggets they uncover". The processual view also stresses that city government does not carry out the knowledge city strategy, but that it builds governance structures and influences networks capable of carrying out it. City government intervenes and, if effective, then withdraws. The art of strategic change is therefore wherever possible to work with the powers and strengths existing in a city, for to work against them uses energy in often frustrating endeavours.

The studies related to strategic planning in the promotion of urban and regional development usually deal with problems like *why* actions happen or should be happening, and *what* is planned to be done in the planning process prior to the actual decision-making. However, it is as important to analyse *how* these things are being done, in and beyond strategic planning. Hence, the quality of the process emerges as an important issue, and with it the question of how to combine possible, imaginable and probable futures into our every day actions in a continuous learning process forms the core of strategy work. This leads attention on learning processes to prevent development processes ending up with intolerable fragmentation, where the future is always trampled by the issues of a moment, tensioned issues and actors in competition. In this kind of approach, the key questions revolve around trust, communication and learning (Figure 7.2), and generative leaders are in search for answers, for example, to following questions: how is information flow organised between key actors of the influence networks, what blocks the information flow? What is the "value added" that each of the actors brings in the process? How do various actors commit themselves to an interactive process? Why do they commit or why they do not? How is institutional learning enabled, how is feedback transformed to action in the interactive development process? In what formal and informal forums are strategies designed, implemented, revised and discussed? How is such trust created and maintained that enables critical discussion about strategies, fresh views on them and the role of various organisations? How can the interactive development process be organised so that division of labour between organisations is as clear as possible and the process can be kept flowing without being too fixed in a continuous argumentative carrousel? The core idea is that generative leaders work to facilitate the iterative cycle of communication, learning and trust, which should produce new knowledge, improve competencies and construct collective beliefs. Ultimately, this kind of iterative process should increase perseverance and consistency in action. All this improves strategic adaptive capacity (resilience), believes a processualist.

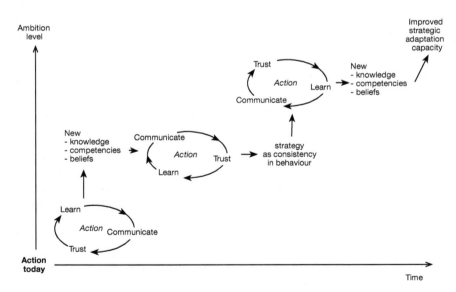

Figure 7.2 Simplified illustration of the ideal of processual strategy development

According to processualists, what matters in strategy is the long-term construction and consolidation of the distinctive internal competencies in the city and its many organisations and networks. From this perspective, strategy becomes a patient inwardly conscious process that simultaneously stresses experience, internal competencies, multi-voice communication and constant learning. Applying Whittington, we can find four points where this approach differs radically from the classical perspective: first, strategy may be a decision-making heuristic, a device to simplify reality into something policy-makers can actually cope with; second, plans may be just security blankets for policy-makers, providing reassurance as much as guidance; third, strategy does not necessarily precede action but may only emerge retrospectively, once the action has taken place; and fourth, strategy is not just about choosing markets or clusters (i.e. identifying what to focus on and then policing performance), but is also about carefully cultivating internal competencies to continuously find new opportunities and adapting swiftly. Many of the basic premises of classicists are put in jeopardy. As Whittington puts it: "suddenly, it seems that goals are slippery and vague, long-term policy statements vain delusion, and the separation of formulation from implementation a self-serving top management myth" (Whittington, 1993: 27).

As stated above, most of what has been written about strategy deals with how it should be designed or systematically formulated. However, as we have seen, strategy is both formulated and emergent, and planning cannot always generate truly innovative new strategies. Strategy may be a good tool in the hands of a skilful generative leader, but not an element in a strategy making cycle of an influence network. Classical strategic planning is rooted in scientific thinking, and if policy-makers are locked into a too instrumental view and an illusion of the objectiveness of their activities, development practitioners will be left, as Forester (1993) states, "all too often as frustrated Machiavellians, technicians, or rule-mongering bureaucrats" (see also Padt, 2012). We need to acknowledge that strategic planning is also a tool in power games between key actors. It may be a way to stabilise the power relations, include or exclude some of the actors, and a means to direct the attention of other players towards the front instead of real issues. Therefore, generative leadership suggests that we should not only ask whether the planning procedure has created a unique strategy with a compelling vision, but whether the strategy process enhanced collaboration, penetrated social filters and hence also influenced the construction of collective beliefs and boosted communication patterns.

In the case of the Helsinki Metropolitan Area, the question of whether the strategic planning process has enhanced the development efforts, created new collaboration patterns in a "triple helix" constellation and hence collective learning cycles differ to some extent between the main dimensions. To cut a long story short, the overall picture of the strategy's role in boosting collaboration is as follows (the statement in the survey and the share of respondents agreeing with it are presented):

- The strategy process was a good forum for discussions and collective contemplation (91.7% agreed with the statement).

- The strategy process increased understanding about the other organisations and thus created fertile soil for future collaboration (89.8% agreed).
- The strategy process enabled people to get rid of daily routines and have time for collective future-oriented contemplation (81.7% agreed).
- The strategy process has strengthened personal-level networks (69.1% agreed).
- The strategy process fostered collaboration between universities and firms (62% agreed).
- The strategy process fostered collaboration between universities and municipalities (60.6% agreed).
- The strategy process fostered collaboration between universities (58.8% agreed).
- The strategy process fostered collaboration between firms (57.4% agreed).
- The strategy process fostered collaboration between firms and municipalities (57.0% agreed).
- The strategy process fostered collaboration between universities and state agencies (50.5% agreed).

As the figures indicate, strategy development is a means of fostering collaboration but it also is a means of encouraging communication, that is, messages from one group of actors to another. Of the respondents, 89.8% perceived that the innovation strategy enabled the HMA to construct a shared message about the area and its future potential as well as to transmit it onwards, and 69.1% thought that the innovation strategy is a useful tool for sharpening the marketing efforts of the entire metropolitan area. In spite of these positive views, only half of the respondents thought that the key message of the strategy had been disseminated widely in the area or beyond. At all events, it is possible to conclude that the strategic planning process served the creation of a core message to be marketed fairly well. Outward-orientated message construction had progressed well and according to the participants internal learning was an even more significant outcome of the process. As many as 70% of the respondents agreed with the statement that strategy work boosted individual-level learning. Additionally, an increased collective strategic awareness as well as a shared vocabulary was enhanced during the process that enabled key actors to better understand and discuss emerging issues. For its part, the fresh conceptual framework enabled collaboration and the finding of targets for development efforts. All this suggests, as 70.6% of the respondents maintained, that the cognitive gap between various stakeholders narrowed with shared awareness and vocabulary and that this, if sustainable, may be good news for future collaboration.

The above views on strategy as a learning and collaboration-oriented process acknowledge at the outset many of the shortcomings faced in classical strategic planning, but at the same time there is a danger of going too far, a danger of falling into the trap of the processual strategy. **The trap of the processual strategy** is based on too well established **belief** that: (a) the continuous strategy process would be able to create its future paths by itself without adequate attention to inventing and proposing possible and probable futures; (b) it would be possible to flexibly and rapidly react and adapt to the surprises of the turbulent environment without adequate foresight as well as strategic analyses and planning and; (c) at the grassroots level new strategic initiatives and intentions would grow continuously that benefit the whole without adequate support and guidance from the top.

If one sinks into the processual strategy trap, one believes too much in the prevailing system, and many potential and necessary societal innovations may easily be covered by the daily fuss of conflicts, problems, meetings, appointments and so on, and probable and possible future options are not easily seen and the interconnections between daily actions and the emergence of the future fails to be identified. The danger of falling into the black hole of the processual strategy is as big as the one of falling into the black hole of classical strategy. Therefore, generative leaders need also to use the methods of the classical strategic planning in their efforts to direct processual strategy development. The trick is to find a proper place for classical strategic planning and not to overemphasise its role. A tentative and partial answer to the question posed above – what do we need strategies for – can be given:

- To avoid the trap of the classical strategic planning we need the characteristics of the processual approach to emphasise communication, trust, learning, bargaining and negotiations as continuous features of city development (i.e. process qualities).
- To avoid the trap of the processual strategy we need methods and analyses of classical strategic planning to enable us to stop the process and the daily fuss associated with it, and to provide actors with the possibility of discussing strategic issues, their own intentions and the probable and possible futures of the respective city-region, and thus construct strategic awareness and collective beliefs (i.e. factual basis for strategy).

7.5 One or many strategies – what roles for strategy?

Economic development strategies of a city are supposed to guide the activities of many organisations involved in the influence networks, but in practice it seems to be clear and only natural that different organisations participate in strategy making in order to ensure that their own needs and the ideas of their backers are included in the strategies, thereby safeguarding their own territory, and also in order to see what notions are uppermost in the minds of assigned leaders. Development strategies of cities are all too often seen as one of the fields of opportunity for maximising one"s own interests, rather than a new context in which actors share strategies for the good of the entire city. The challenge is that generative leaders ought to be able to serve the needs of the many players, firms, universities, local communities, and so forth, but simultaneously, they should allow powerful firms and other organisations to influence the process but not allow them to hijack the agenda for their own short-term gain.

It is worth repeating that networks and classical strategies do not go particularly well together, as classical strategic planning does not enable us to make a long term and enduring combination of different action logics and the differing strategies and objectives emerging from these. In such a "system", process rather than organisation is the key to strategic success (MacNeill and Steiner, 2010). The assumption that collaboration can be achieved within city strategies is hard to implement, but if we accept that organisations and individuals are selfish and always approach city development from their own point of view, we could make an assumption that **true collaboration is achievable between individual strategies but not within a collective one**. When collaboration is achieved between strategies, cognitive diversity is accepted, as well as the options for cooperation and conflict arising from it. The point of departure, therefore, is that the promotion of knowledge city development through strategies is by nature more political than technocratic, and the search for the theoretical bases of strategic planning and the concrete forms of it are pursued in the direction of the processual and communicative features of strategy too. During a continuous process, the various goals and strategies of individual organisations are made as parallel as possible by inter-organisational learning, communication and negotiation but also classical strategic planning. Here, the mission of the formulation of local strategies is not to guide different actors directly, but to be itself the arena for discussions, battles and quarrels (cf. Healey, 1992).

Consequently, in the hands of skilful generative leaders, whoever they are, strategy development may be a powerful tool for exercising and gaining inter-pretive and network power, and it ought to be studied and developed as such. In this kind of setting, as Healey points out, the critical intent should not be directed at the discourses of the different participants (it should not be "we are right and you are wrong") but at the discourse around the specific actions being *invented* through the communicative process. Thus, shaping and organising attention, formulating and reformulating problems and opportunities, addressing significance and leading belief formation will, among other things, emerge as crucial. In a way, a "local knowledge strategy" is a sequence of choices made by many independent actors, and a collective strategy process can be seen as a quest for strategic collaboration, awareness building and the construction of collective beliefs. The question is about boosting development work by finding natural touch points between the strategies and visions of many organisations, rather than about having one strategy for many actors. The earlier tentative and partial answer to why we need strategies can now be expanded. Strategy development is a many-sided tool that has at least the following direct and indirect direction-setting functions and roles in collective development efforts:

- A strategy may be a **classical plan**, in which a vision, strategies and adequate measures are presented in order to channel and direct the use of resources.
- The formal strategy process may provide actors with legitimate **arenas** for collaboration.

- A strategy process may be a conscious effort to penetrate a social filter and **construct collective beliefs**, to **learn a common language** and new concepts, and to create shared lines of action and strategic awareness, as well as a way of seeing the development and the role of various actors in it. Therefore, strategy development is also about tools for rehearsing futures.
- The intended strategy may be a means of communication, that is, **messages** from one group of actors to another group.
- The strategy process may be a tool for making better sense of the ongoing open **social discourse** in a city from the point of view of global developments.

Table 7.1 presents both the basic assumptions regarding classical strategic planning and the basic assumptions derived from process-oriented generative leadership. The classical assumptions reflect a particularly strong belief in the ability of individuals to identify and create new strategies and see new competitive advantages. Diversity and the need for continuous strategic adaptation, however, are hard to manage within classical strategy making. What is essential is to perceive strategic planning as a part of a continuous process, as a moment in the flow of action and development.

Table 7.1 Basic assumptions of classical strategic planning and strategy as a tool for generative leaders

Classical strategic planning	*Generative leadership and strategy*
Strategy development based on shared vision and shared strategies – strategic action within a shared strategy.	Strategy development based on making the strategies of individual actors parallel – strategic action *between strategies* of individual actors.
Several organisation's decision-making and activity directed by collective strategies.	Formulation of a local strategy is an arena for discussion, negotiation and conflict. It is one of the arenas for the construction of strategic awareness and collective beliefs. Strategic planning is a way to create a distance from the everyday toil and effort in order to learn collectively.
In strategic planning novel, creative and unique strategies are formulated.	Strategic planning is not only a means to create the intended strategy but to rehearse futures and learn new thinking and vocabulary, and thus create an enduring and fertile soil from which the strategy can emerge.
Strategies are formulated ready-made in the planning process – planning and implementation are separate.	Strategy is not a plan but a leadership tool with many dimensions.

Note

1   There were 111 respondents altogether, of which 86 are men and 25 women. The majority (69%) belong to the top management of their organisations and 17.4% to the middle management. The rest of the respondents are either engaged with operative and/or project work (3.7%). Most of the respondents work for various private organisations (44.5%) and local government (33.6%). The rest come from various state agencies (10.9%), universities (6.4%) and polytechnics (4.5%). Most of the respondents had participated in strategy making (65.8%).

8 Did we learn something?

Generative leadership, strategic intentions and emergence

Leadership is stressed in this book but it is important to keep in mind that no study has revealed a causal relationship between leaders and changes in local/regional development (Leach and Wilson, 2002). Indeed, knowledge cities cannot be created overnight linearly with one "super leader" who solves all problems and satisfies all interests (Termeer and Nooteboom, 2012) – at its best leadership is a shared effort that is developed over long periods and embedded both in governance structures and informal, often "invisible", factors that facilitate trusting relationships and collaboration between leaders and other local players (Karlsen and Larrea, 2012). Generative leadership is a systemic but not a personal quality, and as such it is more about a process and network relationships than individuals only. This again reminds that leadership is embedded in the social fabric of the place and the wider governance systems. Drawing upon on a series of case studies Sotarauta *et al.* (2012) conclude that leadership is a process, in which socially embedded indirect influence is the core, and hence the need to understand what individuals do in their specific places to induce development ought to be of interest also in local and regional economic development.

This books needs to be read as a proposition, a proposition of how to approach leadership in knowledge city development. It proposes that there is a need to reach beyond seeing leaders only as actors who lead the authorities or organisations assigned to them. In city development, we may gain new insights and analytical leverage if we aim at identifying actors who lead networks and processes instead of pre-defined structures. Generative leaders often are social inventors and pioneers who venture into unexplored territories and guide other people to new and often unfamiliar destinations. They are going before and showing the way, but we should acknowledge that there are many ways to do all this, and that our knowledge of the ways in which generative leadership is exercised in different parts of the world is very limited. Often, leaders act as thought leaders and boundary spanners, and they are concerned with building the networks, structures and mental models for the future; that is, they aim to secure new resources and develop new capabilities, and by those means position the city and its organisations to take advantage of emerging opportunities and adapt strategically to change. To repeat the main message:

- Generative leaders are leaders, as *they stretch constraints* while managers operate within them.
- Generative leaders reach beyond their familiar fields of activity and policy spheres to influence. They reach beyond those individual organisations and institutions that authorise them to take the lead in the first place.
- Generative leaders are required to influence actors who are not by definition their followers, and conversely, followers are not assigned to them; to take a leadership position in an influence network calls for good capabilities in earning the position, in a situation where followers always have a choice not to act and follow.
- Generative leadership, and the process view it draws upon, is about living and coping with emergence and not about aiming to control.

Generative leadership is far from a linear and straightforward act of influencing. It is characterised by (a) fragmented and/or shared actions, events and incidents among a whole series of organisations and/or several leaders, rather than processes that simply flow from "top down" from some kind of a control centre to followers; (b) processes where not all people who are leaders are formally recognised as such (while sometimes people with formal positions may exercise only little if no leadership at all); and (c) multi-scalar, dynamic and interactive governance processes between national, local and regional government actors, firms, universities, research institutions, public and/or semi-public development agencies. So, this book proposes that to understand generative leadership it is essential to understand and explain how actors influence each other in constructing collective beliefs and agreement on that which needs to be done and how, and how they move from thinking to action and back. All too often in urban and regional economic development literature, the promotion of economic development is approached simply as a policy issue. Of course, as reminded in the introductory chapter, history makes leaders who are mere pawns in the riptide of socio-politico-economic forces, but there are also leaders who direct the evolution of their cities, in collaboration with other actors. In doing so, they not only formulate plans and manoeuvre to change the complex governance systems but they focus on people, which is what leadership is all about.

Generative leadership aims to show the way for a variety of actors; but hence, we face a dilemma. The leading idea of leadership and strategic planning is often that it might be possible to find a best fit between the strategic intentions of large groups of actors and the emergent forces. In the muddled and complex networks aiming to promote city development on the one hand, and in the midst of emergent development patterns on the other, it may be hard, if not impossible, to find the best fit. Aiming for strategies with the best fit may result in actors being overly conservative in situations where novel solutions are needed and novel strategies ought to be invented and explored. However, these are exactly the reasons why generative leaders should accept different organisations and groups promoting city development from their own perspectives. They should accept the differences between their visions, and their different goals and strategies. At the same time they ought to be able to see the diversity of strategic intentions, and the many reasons for joining the influence networks and making a commitment. It is clear that most of the central actors in city development are not interested in contributing to the local economic development efforts but in securing their own future success.

In contemporary governance thinking, leadership is no longer about "giving strategic orders" or using institutional power only; therefore, if strategy is still seen as classical plan-making, the outcome easily becomes the divorce of strategy formulation from the process of implementation, which is always dependent on independent organisations and a range of different partners. Generative leaders should therefore not assume too readily that, once formulated, strategies are automatically subject to implementation, or that they are a source of influence; rather, they should see the many-sided nature of development strategies and use them in their act of leading. To overcome the dilemmas embedded in generative leadership and its use of strategic planning, there is a need to approach strategy as a two-way process. As Mintzberg (1994) states, deliberate strategies are not necessarily good, and emergent strategies are not necessarily bad. Thus, strategies are both designed and emergent. Both qualities are needed, since every development effort by necessity combines some degree of flexible learning with some degree of cerebral control. Therefore, instead of a grand plan, strategy can basically be seen as a guiding pattern for the ever-flowing stream of single actions and decisions. It gathers them under the same "umbrella" and leads them in the desired direction. According to this definition, strategy is consistency in behaviour, whether intended or not. Strategic planning can be used as a mirror to guide consistency of behaviour, and to make emergence a little bit more intentional.

In the knowledge city context, commitment to strategic intentions seems to have a new content; no commitment is necessarily sought for the ready-made ideas in the strategic planning process. There is rather a constant search for commitment from different points of view for shared processes requiring and enabling commitment. It is expected that the players commit to playing the game instead of *a priori* planned outcome; constant search for strategies and means to improve the situation. Of course, every now and then concrete projects emerge that call for financial or other tangible forms of commitment in the planning phase. But, fundamentally, the strategy continues to live and change along with circumstances and sets of actors. In a way, strategies are constantly being recreated, and their direction quite often emerges through communication and interpretive processes. A development strategy is therefore the result of several strategic intentions being aligned in time and the continuous adjustment to surprises caused by emergent forces. And here is the crucial point, being processual in nature, it is easier to open the development processes for various stakeholders and let the strategy emerge, not for the people and firms, but with and by them – this kind of "distributed intelligence" may be the strongest possible way to adapt strategically to emergent forces. Utilisation of this kind of approach needs generative leadership that values strategy as a craft, as an art.

It follows that shared strategic intentions are in practice combinations of the goals and visions of individual actors, and therefore, an ability to identify individual goals and to find and create the common denominators – the "third solutions" – between them seems to be a prerequisite for shared strategic intentions. Shared strategic intention is based on imagining the future between visions, in which appreciating "other visions" is crucial, and learning about other actors' thinking patterns and especially their views and perceptions of futures forms the core skill of a generative leader. What often appears as collective action is in practice a complex, constantly evolving process between an influence network and its members that generative leaders try to lead.

The idea of generative leadership suits the knowledge city development rather well as it exploits the gap between unattainable goals and resources – that is easy to achieve, the kind of situation being the normal condition in most of the cities. Cities are usually faced with the endless flow of demands directed at development strategies that exceed available resources. The idea of generative leadership suggests using this phenomenon to benefit the development games by challenging the networks, and not letting scarce resources suppress thinking and the development efforts. Strategic intention sets expectations that challenge personal effort and commitment. The emphasis is on leveraging resources to reach seemingly unattainable goals, whereas the traditional view of strategy focuses on the degree of fit between existing resources and current opportunities; strategic intention creates an extreme misfit between resources and ambitions. Generative leadership then challenges a city and its many actors to close the gap by

Table 8.1 Strategic intentions in generative leadership and the reactive adaptation

	Reactive adaptation	*Generative leadership*
Rules of the game	Leaders identify the existing rules of the game and adapt to them.	Leaders search for new rules of the game and exploit them, but also influence their emergence and shape the existing ones.
Competencies	Leaders focus on identifiable targets for development, e.g. existing clusters.	Leaders construct portfolio of competencies in networks to meet the emergent and unexpected forces.
Learning	Leaders enhance collective learning for specialisation.	Leaders enhance collective learning to meet the emergent and unexpected.
Advantage	Leaders find competitive advantage based on existing resources, networks and knowledge.	Leaders construct novel advantages based on new knowledge, networks and resources.
Resources and ambitions	Leaders match ambitions to existing resources.	Leaders leverage new resources by searching for new ambitions through imagining the futures between visions.
Objective	Leaders meet the financial targets.	Leaders challenge actors and networks with bold intentions.

systematically constructing new advantages. Strategic intention is an obsession with creating space that is off the traditional map and that allows an entire city to adapt strategically to emergent forces. Generative leadership is therefore *futures seeking*, but not, like most classical methods, *future defining*. Generative leaders build on strategic intentions to avoid being unconsciously curtailed by what they see, who they know and what they can measure, and they avoid falling into the black holes of the classical and processual approaches. Generative leadership needs to be grounded in innovative ideas, which are not to be found in reactive adaptation, but need to be invented (Table 8.1).

Conceptual epilogue

Generative leaders excite people; they find ways to make people work for the city but also to strengthen their own position. Generative leaders often are the glue that keeps collaboration together, and they open new horizons in collective thinking. This is the ideal, a scarce "natural resource" in many cities, a hard to identify feature of city development.

The concept of generative leadership reminds us that in knowledge cities, there are endless series of specific projects and processes that give the directions to overall development, and that, in many places, both visible and invisible hands shepherd people to novel directions. "Invisible hand" does not here refer only to Adam Smith's description of how unintended social benefits result from individual actions but also to those actors who influence how we think and collaborate, and who work to change the rules of the game. This again leads us to raise a few ingredients, not all of which have been explicitly dealt with in the previous chapters, but which have been present implicitly throughout the book. These are: creative tension, sense of urgency, ambitious story and inductive strategy. In short, generative leaders find ways to generate creative tension that excites people, they understand the importance of a sense of urgency, they prefer ambitious and believable stories to technically perfect plans in spite of valuing highly the factual evidence base, and instead of aiming to construct a shared vision they lead by continuously searching for shared visions among the individual visions. It might not be an exaggeration to say that generative leaders are masters of inductive and inducing strategies (see also Sotarauta and Kosonen, 2004).

Creative tension genuinely inspires people to become involved in collective efforts. "Tension" refers here to intense anxiety that makes actors feel something is stretching them, taking them into unknown situations and environments. This kind of tension may become creative and lead to the invention of something new, or it may become disruptive and lead to undesired outcomes. Generative leaders often generate tension to make social filters quiver, and they take pains to lead anxiety towards something creative. Hence, creative tension refers to the excitement that emerges from uncertainty about the consequences of future events and measures, and from the dominating thought and/or action patterns questioned by forces which are in mutual opposition or sufficiently different from one another. Creative tension may challenge actors in unprecedented ways, leading to original products or processes, thoughts and action models. Creative tension may come into being spontaneously or as a result of leadership. Creative tension is important as it feeds into *the sense of urgency*; in other words, generative leadership relays need the sense of drama and the feeling of progress and excitement. A sense of urgency adds energy and commitment to the process. Sometimes, it may be that formal strategic planning processes or large pots of European funding may provide actors with a false sense of security instead of emphasising the need to invest one's own time and money in creativity and innovation.

To create a sense of urgency, the generative leadership relay requires an *ambitious and believable storyline* that is collectively debated and constructed and that thus becomes the directing force that reaches beyond individual actors, plans and/or strategies. Through a believable story, it is possible to link fragmented pieces of information as well as intentions and interests together, in a world that is full of information and filled with competing ideas and interests, not to mention local development programmes, projects and other development efforts. To do this, leaders need to provide a context for the action and a storyline that gives meaning to the action, and it is exactly here where vision is useful. Actors need to comprehend the purpose of adaptive or transformative measures so that they focus less on the persons, and what they already know and more on the meaning of the new action. For its part, an ambitious and believable story builds *strategic awareness* that is the basis for collective beliefs and which feeds back into the storyline. In a generative leadership relay, construction of a collective strategy is not so much about strategic plans and shared visions as it is about the generation of collective strategic awareness that, if everything goes well, is the basis for collective belief formation. Awareness calls for a well-established ability to monitor and interpret various global developments and local events and to make sense of them. Awareness becomes strategic with the ability to find the strategic issues in relation to a given development game. And when strategic awareness is collectively constructed, so too is the capacity to carry the development game and keep the leadership relay in motion. Long-term strategies exist not so much on paper but in the fibre and thinking of the key actors. As the two generative leadership relay cases show in Chapter 7, strategy is as much inductive as it is deductive; it bounces back and forth.

A sense of urgency born out of creative tension and fed by an ambitious and believable story is not always guided by a shared vision, as is often assumed, but by the capacity to bring forth a *shared vision among individual visions – to imagine futures between visions*. That which often appears to be a collective action is, in practice, a complex, constantly evolving process between an influence network and its members; that is, a local development game carried forward by a leadership relay. It is often argued that city development requires intensive collaboration and collective action, and here it is argued that a leadership relay pushes forward collective action over time and across various obstacles, and that collective action calls for actors who can create a sense of urgency by the creative tension that emerges among visions rather than from within one vision. All of this also challenges classical notions of designed strategies and suggests that in leadership relays we can also find *inductive and inducing strategies* that are wrapped in a constantly emerging storyline. Collective interpretation and belief formation are often among the core processes in a leadership relay. It is again worth stressing that, in inducing strategy based on continuously shaped storylines, the question is not about having a ready-made plot but about a constantly emerging and ongoing discussion that bounces back and forth between the visions and practical issues, and between many organisations.

Generative leaders live with their cities, influence networks and development strategies, and mould them, and are being moulded, as they go.

Appendix 1

The questionnaire used to identify resources of power and influence tactics used in the local and regional development champions – actual and aspirational generative leaders (Sotarauta *et al.*, 2007)

(1) In regional development it is important to induce many actors to become part of collective development efforts. Assess from your own work point of view, what measures are important when you aim to influence other actors for regional development (all statements on Likert scale from not important at all [1] to fairly important [3] to very important [5])

Constructing an atmosphere of trust   _____

Acting as a role model for other actors so that they would work also for development instead of focusing solely on their own organisations   _____

Creating a vision to guide development activities of several actors   _____

Channelling development funds controlled by my own development agency   _____

Organising development work so that the roles of individual actors are clear   _____

Increasing the level of expertise by organising education   _____

Organising collective strategy making processes   _____

Removing communication obstacles between actors   _____

Arbitrating conflicts that complicate development work   _____

Affecting general atmosphere via media   _____

Delegating one's own responsibility to other actors   _____

Raising differing viewpoints and bottlenecks into the development-oriented discourse   _____

Getting other actors out of their comfort zone by provocation   _____

Encouraging other actors in public speeches and/or written pieces   _____

Influencing other actors by production of new information   _____

Presenting alternative views on futures, and promotion of regional development, thus influencing other actors   _____

Binding functional relationships with influential persons   _____
Activating new actors to participate in the official development work   _____
Organising open communication sessions   _____
Discussing with other actors before renewing one's own strategy   _____
Invoking the sense or responsibility of the key-actors   _____
Invoking legislation and/or official development programmes   _____
Providing other actors with new opportunities   _____
Providing other actors with expert help   _____

What is missing, what other measures might be important?

_____

_____

_____

_____

(2) Assess from the point of view of your own work and practice what factors are important in your personal efforts to influence other actors for regional development (all statements on Likert scale from not important at all [1] to fairly important [3] to very important [5])

Such expert knowledge that enables me to convince the key
    persons of changes needed   _____
Such personal networks that provide me with new information   _____
Official position that provides me with power to demand that other
    actors act differently   _____
Official position that provides me with power to change institutions
    guiding development work   _____
Good relationships with representatives of the media   _____
Enough time and money to achieve objectives set for me   _____
Authority to reward other actors for work done for the region   _____
New concepts, models and thinking patterns that make other actors
    see things differently   _____
Power to decide how regional development funds are used   _____
Respect of the other actors towards my expertise   _____
Such personal networks that enable me to pull initiatives through _____
Official position that provides me with authority to organise
    official strategy processes   _____
Official position that provides me with authority to change the
    ways the development work is organised   _____
Such expert knowledge that enables me to convince the key
    persons of my own role in the development work   _____

What else?

_____

_____

_____

_____

(3) How do following factors affect your work? (All statements on Likert scale from not at all [1] to very much [5])

There is not enough time to do everything that needs to be done _____
There are not enough funds _____
I do not have enough good partners in my region _____
I do not have enough good partners outside my region _____
My own organisation does not support my development actions _____
Most of the actors concentrate on safeguarding their own interests
    instead of active collaboration _____
There is no new thinking, we are locked into old thinking patterns _____
Old organisational structures make my work difficult _____
The strategy of my organisation is unclear and hence collaboration
    with other actors is difficult _____
Struggle for power make regional development efforts difficult _____
The regional development system is too fragmented _____
Regional development agencies are too small _____
Regional entities according to which regional development policy
    is organised are too small _____
There is no proper vision and strategy to guide the regional
    development activity _____
We are not able to obtain new resources external to our region _____
We are not able to direct the activities and competences of various
    organisations so that they will support regional development
    as well as we would like them to do _____
There are no proper resources in our region we could utilise in our
    development work _____
The regional development system is overly bureaucratic and the
    actual development work is, thus, difficult _____
There are too many project-based employees _____

(6) What kind of organisation you are working in

1. A municipality or some other local organisation _____
2. Sub-regional development organisation _____

3. Regional council   _____
4. Employment and economic development centre   _____
5. Research and/or educational organisation   _____
6. Technology centre   _____
7. A ministry or another kind of national level organisation _____
8. Other, what?

_____

_____

_____

_____

Questions focusing on the backgrounds of the respondents are not included.

Appendix 2

The questionnaire used to identify
the roles of strategic planning in
the Helsinki Metropolitan Area
(all questions used Likert scale from
1 to 5) (Sotarauta and Saarivirta 2012)

Strategic awareness

1. How much did the formulation of the innovation strategy affect your awareness of the importance of developing local innovation systems?
2. Did the innovation strategy help you to understand in what ways global knowledge economy affects local innovation systems?
3. How much did the formulation of the innovation strategy influence your understanding of the competiveness of the Helsinki Metropolitan Area in competition between cities globally?
4. Did formulation of the innovation strategy help you to identify the resources that are crucial in the future development of the local innovation system in the Helsinki Metropolitan Area?

Collaboration and communication

5. How much did the strategic planning process influence collaboration between the following actors?

   a) collaboration between universities
   b) collaboration between universities and the local government
   c) collaboration between universities and firms
   d) collaboration between universities and the state agencies
   e) collaboration between firms
   f) collaboration between firms and the local government
   g) collaboration between firms and the state agencies
   h) collaboration between municipalities
   i) collaboration between the local government and the state agencies

6. Did strategic planning serve well as a forum for joint discussions?

7. Did the formulation of innovation strategy help you to better understand the thinking, objectives and needs of other actors?
8. Did strategic planning surface the pitfalls of collaboration between the main players of the local innovation system?
9. Did strategic planning strengthen the individual level networks?
10. Did strategic planning allow the main actors to stop the daily process and contemplate together the main issues and challenges of the Helsinki Metropolitan Area?

Message

11. Did strategic planning and the new strategy enhance identification of the joint message of the innovation policy network and its transmission to the main stakeholders?
12. Has the strategic plan been disseminated widely and are the strategies and visions of the Helsinki Metropolitan Area now better known than before the strategic planning process?
13. Did strategic planning construct a story line that is shared by the main actors?
14. Has the innovation strategy been useful in the branding and marketing of the Helsinki Metropolitan Area?

Language and development view

15. Did strategic planning support collective learning?
16. Did strategic planning lead to a joint conceptual basis, a vocabulary that allows more elaborated discussions of the competitiveness and the local innovation system than before the planning process?
17. Did the strategic planning align the development views and strategies of the participants?

Vision

18. Did strategic planning construct a shared strategic intention in the Helsinki Metropolitan Area?
19. Did strategic planning construct a shared vision for the Helsinki Metropolitan Area?
20. Are the intended strategies and the vision compelling and challenging?
21. Did strategic planning construct jointly accepted views over the main lines of development?
22. Was strategic planning a good tool in identification of the most important targets of collective development efforts?
23. Did the strategy channel resources to the most important targets of development work?
24. Did strategic planning lead to identification of concrete means to strengthen the local innovation system?

25. Did strategic planning initiate new collective development efforts?
26. Did strategic planning identify the major pitfalls in the local innovation system?
27. Did strategic planning support perseverant and consistent construction of local innovation system
28. Did strategic planning concretise blue-sky thinking and bold but abstract ideas?
29. Was strategic planning a useful process?
30. Did strategic planning remain at such an abstract level that it does not serve actual development work?
31. Did the participants in the strategic planning process understand each other's vocabulary and thinking?
32. How intensively did you participate in the strategic planning?

Questions focusing on the backgrounds of the respondents are not included.

References

Agranoff, R. and McGuire, M. (2001) "Big questions in public network management research", *Journal of Public Administration Research and Theory*, 11:3, 295–326.

Alchian, A. A. (1950) "Uncertainty, evolutions and economic theory", *The Journal of Political Economy*, 58:3, 211–21.

Allen J. (2003) *Lost Geographies of Power*. Oxford: Blackwell.

Allen, P. M. (1990) "Why the future is not what it was", *Futures*, 22:6, 555–70.

Amin, A. (2001) "Moving on: Institutionalism in economic geography", *Environment and Planning A*, 33:7, 1237–1241.

Asheim, B. T., Boschma, R., Cooke, P., Laredo, P., Lindholm-Dahlstrand, Å. and Piccaluga, A. (2006) *Constructing Regional Advantage: Principles, perspectives and policies* (final report). Brussels: DG Research, European Commission.

Asheim, B. T., Moodysson, J. and Tödtling, F. (2011) "Special issue: Constructing regional advantage: Towards state-of-the-art regional innovation system policies in Europe?" *European Planning Studies*, 19:7, 1203–1219.

Association of Finnish Local and Regional Authorities, *Local and Regional Government Finland: Finnish local government*. Available at: www.localfinland.fi/en/association/research/newmunicipality2017/Documents/Finnish-Local-Government.pdf (accessed 23 April 2015).

Axelrod, R. (1997) *The Complexity of Cooperation: Agent-based models of competition and collaboration*. Princeton, NJ: Princeton University Press.

Bailey, D., Bellandi, M., Caloffi, A. and De Propris, L. (2010) "Place-renewing leadership: Trajectories of change for mature manufacturing regions in Europe", *Policy Studies*, 31:4, 457–74.

Barber, A. and Montserrat, P. (2010) "Leadership challenges in the inner city: Planning for sustainable regeneration in Birmingham and Barcelona", *Policy Studies*, 31:4, 393–411.

Bass, B. M. (1991) "From transactional to transformational leadership: Learning to share the vision", *Organizational Dynamics*, 18:3, 19–31.

Bass, B. M. and Bass, R. (2008) *The Bass Handbook of Leadership: Theory, research, and managerial applications* (4th edn). New York: Free Press.

Bass, B. M. and Riggio, R. E. (2006) *Transformational Leadership*. Mahwah, NJ: Lawrence Erbaum Associates.

Bathelt, H. and Glückler, J. (2003) "Toward a relational economic geography", *Journal of Economic Geography*, 3:2, 117–44.

Bathelt, H., Malmberg, A. and Maskell, P. (2004) "Clusters and knowledge: Local buzz, global pipelines and the process of knowledge creation", *Progress in Human Geography*, 28:1, 31–56.

Battilana J., Leca, B. and Boxenbaum, E. (2009) "How actors change institutions: Towards a theory of institutional entrepreneurship", *The Academy of Management Annals*, 3:1, 65–107

Beer, A. (2014) "Leadership and the governance of rural communities", *Journal of Rural Studies*, 34, 254–62.

Beer, A. and Baker, E. (2012) "Adaptation, adjustment, and leadership in Australia's rural margins". In Sotarauta, M., Horlings, I. and Liddle, J. (eds) *Leadership and Change in Sustainable Regional Development* (pp. 103–120). Abingdon, UK: Routledge.

Beer, A. and Clower, T. (2014) "Mobilising leadership in cities and regions", *Regional Studies, Regional Science*, 1:1, 10–34.

Bennett, N., Wise C., Woods, P. A. and Harvey, J. A. (2003) *Distributed Leadership: A review of literature*. London: National College for School Leadership/The Open University.

Benneworth, P. S. (2004) "In what sense 'regional development'? Entrepreneurship, underdevelopment and strong tradition in the periphery", *Entrepreneurship and Regional Development*, 16:6, 437–58.

Benneworth, P. S. (2007) *Leading Innovation: Building effective regional coalitions for innovation* (Research report). London: Nesta.

Benneworth, P. S., Charles, D. R. and Madnipour, A. (2010) "Universities as agents of urban change in the global knowledge economy", *European Planning Studies*, 18:10, 1611–1630.

Benneworth, P. S., Pinheiro, R. and Karlsen, J. (forthcoming) "Strategic agency and institutional change: Investigating the role of universities in Regional Innovation Systems (RISs)", *Regional Studies.*

Bennis, W. (1999) "The leadership advantage", *Leader to Leader*, 12, 18–23.

Bentley, G., Pugalis, L. and Shutt, J. (forthcoming) "Leadership and systems of governance: The constraints on the scope for leadership of place-based development in sub-national territories", *Regional Studies.*

Bionext (2010) *Innovation for Well-Being 2003–2010*. Tampere, Finland: Bionext.

Blanco, I. (2009) "Does a 'Barcelona Model' really exist? Periods, territories and actors in the process of urban transformation", *Local Government Studies*, 35:3, 355–69.

Blazek, J., Zizalova, P., Rumpel, P., Skokan, K. and Chladek, P. (2013) "Emerging regional innovation strategies in Central Europe: Institutions and regional leadership in generating strategic outcomes", *European Urban and Regional Studies*, 20:2, 275–94.

Brown, N (2003) "Hope against hype: Accountability in biopasts, presents and future", *Science Studies*, 16:2, 3–21.

Bruun, H. (2002) "The emergence of regional innovation network: A process analysis of the local bio-grouping in Turku". In Sotarauta, M. and Bruun, H. (eds) *Nordic Perspectives on Process-Based Regional Development Policy* (pp. 79–124). Nordregio report 2002:3, Stockholm.

Bryson, J. M. and Crosby, B. C. (1992) *Leadership for the Common Good: Tackling public problems in a shared-power world*. San Francisco, CA: Jossey-Bass.

Burfitt, A. and MacNeill, S. (2008) "The challenges of pursuing cluster policy in the congested state", *International Journal of Urban and Regional Research*, 32:2, 492–505.

Campbell, T. (2009) "Learning cities: Knowledge, capacity and competitiveness", *Habitat International*, 33:2, 195–201.

Carillo, F. J. (2006) *Knowledge Cities: Approaches, experiences and perspectives*, Burlington, MA: Butterworth-Heinemann.

Carrillo, F. J., Yititcanlar, T., García, B. and Lönnqvist, A. (2014) *Knowledge and the City: Concepts, applications and trends of knowledge-based urban development*. Abingdon, UK: Routledge.

Castells, M. (1997) *The Power of Identity: The information age: Economy, society and culture*. Oxford: Blackwell.

Charnock, G. and Ribera-Fumaz, R. (2011) "A new space for knowledge and people? Henri Lefebvre, representations of space, and the production of 22@Barcelona", *Environment and Planning D: Society and Space*, 29:4, 613–32.

Chatterton, P. and Hodkinson, S. (2007) "Leeds skyscraper city", *The Yorkshire and Humber Regional Review*. Available at: http://citeseerx.ist.psu.edu/viewdoc/download?doi=10.1.1.184.6780andrep=rep1andtype=pdf (accessed 14 January 2015).

Cho, M. and Hassink, R. (2009) "Limits to locking-out through restructuring: The textile industry in Daegu", *South Korea, Regional Studies*, 43:9, 1183–1198.

Collinge, C. and Gibney, J. (2010a) "Connecting place, policy and leadership", *Policy Studies*, 31:4, 379–91.

Collinge, C. and Gibney, J. (2010b) "Place making and the limitation of spatial leadership: Reflection on the Øresund", *Policy Studies*, 31:4, 475–889.

Collinge, C., Gibney, J. and Mabey, C. (2011) *Leadership and Place*. Abingdon, UK: Routledge.

Cooke, P. (2002) *Knowledge economies: Clusters, Learning and Cooperative Advantage*. London: Routledge.

Cooke, P. and Leysdorff, L. (2006) "Regional development in the knowledge-based economy: The construction of advantage", *The Journal of Technology Transfer*, 31:1, 5–15.

Couto, R. A. (2010) "Introduction". In Couto, R. A. (ed.) *Political and Civic Leadership: A reference handbook* (pp. xv–xx). Thousand Oaks, CA: Sage.

Creswell, T. (2004) *Place: A short introduction*. Oxford: Blackwell.

D'Ovidio, M. and Pradel, M. (2013) "Social innovation and institutionalisation in the cognitive-cultural economy: Two contrasting experiences from Southern Europe", *Cities*, 33, 69–76.

Dahl, R. A. (2005) *Who Governs? Democracy and Power in an American City*. New Haven, CT: Yale University Press.

Degen, M. and Carcía, M. (2012) "The transformation of the 'Barcelona Model': An analysis of culture, urban regeneration and governance", *International Journal of Urban and Regional Research*, 36:5, 1022–1038.

Drori, I. and Landau, D. (2011) *Vision and Change in Institutional Entrepreneurship*. New York: Berghahn Books.

Drucker, P. (1998) *Managing in a Time of Great Change*. New York: Truman Talley Books/Plume.

Dryzeck, J. S. (1993) "Policy analysis and planning: From science to argument". In Fischer, F. and Forester, J. (eds) *The Argumentative Turn in Policy Analysis and Planning* (pp. 213–32). Albany, NY: UCL Press.

Elcock, E. (2001) *Political Leadership*. Cheltenham, UK: Edward Elgar.

Evans, R. (2013) "Harnessing the economic potential of 'second-tier' European cities: Lessons from four different state/urban systems", *Environment and Planning C: Government and Policy*, 33:1, 163–83.

Evans, R. and Karecha, J. (2014) "Staying on top: Why is Munich so resilient and successful?", *European Planning Studies*, 22:5, 1259–1279.

Flanagan, K., Uyarra, U. and Laranja, M. (2011) "Reconceptualising the 'policy mix' for innovation", *Research Policy*, 40:5, 702–13.

Florida, R. (1995) "Toward the learning region", *Futures*, 27:5, 527–36.

Florida, R. (2002) *The Rise of the Creative Class: And how it's transforming work, leisure, community and everyday Life.* New York: Basic Books.

Flyvbjerg, B. (1998) *Rationality and Power: Democracy in practice.* Chicago, IL: University of Chicago Press.

Forester, J. (1993) *Critical Theory, Public Policy and Planning Practice: Towards a critical pragmatism.* Albany, NY: State University of New York Press.

Foucault, M. (1980) *Power/Knowledge: Selected interviews and other writings, 1972–77,* New York: Pantheon Books.

French, J. and Raven, B. H. (1959) "The bases of social power". In Cartwright, D. (ed.) *Studies of Social Power.* Ann Arbor, MI: Institute for Social Research.

Garmann Johnsen, H. C. and Ennals, R. (eds) *Creating Collaborative Advantage: Innovation and knowledge creation in regional economies.* Farnham, UK: Gower.

Gibney, J. (2011a) "Progressive leadership of cities and regions", *European Planning Studies*, 19:4, 613–27.

Gibney, J. (2011b) "Knowledge in a 'shared and interdependent world': Implications for a progressive leadership of cities and regions", *European Planning Studies*, 19:4, 613– 27.

Gibney, J. (2012) "Leadership of place and dynamics of knowledge". In Sotarauta, M., Horlings, I. and Liddle, J. (eds) *Leadership and Change in Sustainable Regional Development* (pp. 20–36). Abingdon, UK: Routledge.

Gibney, J., Copeland, S. and Murie, A. (2009) "Toward a new strategic leadership of place for the knowledge-based economy", *Leadership*, 5:1, 5–23.

Giddens, A. (1984) *The Constitution of Society: Outline of the theory of structuration.* Glasgow: University of California Press.

González, S. and Healey, P. (2005) "A sociological institutionalist approach to the study of innovation in governance capacity", *Urban Studies*, 42:11, 2055–2069.

Gonzalez, S. and Oosterlynck, S. (2014) "Crisis and resilience in a finance-led city: Effects of the global financial crisis in Leeds", *Urban Studies*, 51:15, 3164–3179.

Graen, G. B. and Uhl-Bien, M. (1995) "Relationship-based approach to leadership: Development of leader-member exchange (LMX) theory of leadership over 25 years: Applying a multi-level multi-domain perspective", *The Leadership Quarterly*, 6:2, 219–47.

Grillitsch, M. and Trippl, M. (2013) "Combining knowledge from different sources, channels and geographical scales", *European Planning Studies*, 22:3, 1–21.

Grint, K. (1997) *Leadership Classical, Contemporary, and Critical Approaches.* Oxford: Oxford University Press.

Grint, K. (2001) *The Arts of Leadership.* Oxford: Oxford University Press.

Halkier, H., James, L., Dahlström, M. and Manniche, J. (2012) "Knowledge dynamics and policies for regional development: Towards a new governance paradigm", *European Planning Studies*, 20:11, 1767–1784.

Hambleton, R. (2003) "City leadership and the new public management: A cross national analysis", *National Public Management Research Conference* (Georgetown University, Washington D.C. 9–11 October).

Hambleton, R. and Sweeting, D. (2004) "US-style leadership for English local government?" *Public Administration Review*, 64:4, 474–88.

Harmaakorpi, V. and Niukkanen, H. (2007) "Leadership in different kinds of regional development networks", *Baltic Journal of Management*, 2:1, 80–96.

Harmaakorpi, V., Hermans, R. and Uotila, T. (2009) *Suomalaisen innovaatiojärjestelmän mosaiikki – Alueellisten teemavalintojen tarkastelu*, Discussion Papers, No. 1146. Helsinki, Finland: Elinkeinoelämän Tutkimuslaitos (ETLA).

Hassink, R. (2012) "The end of the learning region as we knew it: Towards learning in space", *Regional Studies*, 46:8, 1055–1066.

Healey, P. (1992) "Planning through debate: The communicative turn in planning theory", *Town Planning Review*, 63:2, 143–62.

Healey, P. (1997) *Collaborative Planning. Shaping Places in Fragmented Societies.* Basingstoke, UK: Macmillan Press.

Healey, P., Cameron, S., Davoudi, S., Graham, S. and Madanipour, A. (1995), "Introduction: The city – crisis, change and invention". In Healey, P., Cameron, S., Davoudi, S., Graham, S. and Madanipour, A. (eds) *Managing Cities* (pp. 1–20). Chichester, UK: John Wiley and Sons.

Healey, P., Madanapour, A. and Magalhaes, C. (1999) "Institutional capacity building, urban planning and urban regeneration projects", *Journal of the Finnish Society for Future Studies*, 18:3, 117–37.

Heifetz, R. A. (1994) *Leadership Without Easy Answers.* Cambridge, MA: The Belknap Press of Harvard University Press.

Heifetz, R. A. (2003) *Leadership Without Easy Answers* (2nd edn). Cambridge, MA: The Belknap Press of Harvard University Press.

Heifetz, R. (2010) "Leadership". In Couto, R. A. (ed.) *Political and Civic Leadership: A reference handbook* (pp. 12–23). Thousand Oaks, CA: Sage.

Hidle, K. and Normann, R. (2013) "Who can govern? Comparing network governance leadership in two Norwegian city regions", *European Planning Studies*, 21:2, 115–30.

Hildreth P. (2011) "What is localism, and what implications do different models have for managing the local economy?", *Local Economy*, 26, 702–14.

Hirst, P. (2000) *Democracy and Governance.* Oxford: Oxford University Press.

Holland, J. (1995) *Hidden Order: How adaptation builds complexity.* New York: Addison Wesley.

Hollands, R. G. (2008) "Will the real smart city please stand up? Intelligent, progressive or entrepreneurial?", *City: Analysis of Urban Trends, Culture, Theory, Policy, Action*, 12:3, 303–20.

Horlings, I. (2012a) "The interplay between social capital, leadership and policy arrangements in European rural regions". In Sotarauta, M., Horlings, I. and Liddle, J. (eds) *Leadership and Change in Sustainable Regional Development* (pp. 121–44). Abingdon, UK: Routledge.

Horlings, I. (2012b) "Value-oriented leadership in the Netherlands". In Sotarauta, M., Horlings, I. and Liddle, J. (eds) *Leadership and Change in Sustainable Regional Development* (252–70). Abingdon, UK: Routledge.

House of Commons Communities and Local Government Committee (2011) *Regeneration: Sixth Report of Session 2010–12*, HC 1014, London: The Stationery Office.

Hu, X. and Hassink, R. (forthcoming) "Place leadership with Chinese characteristics? A case study of the Zaozhuang coal-mining region in transition", *Regional Studies*.

Huxham, C. and Vangen, S. (2000) "Leadership In the shaping and implementation of collaboration agendas: How things happen in a (not quite) joined-up world", *Academy of Management Journal*, 43:6, 1159–1175.

Innes, J. E. and Booher, D. E. (2000) *Network Power in Collaborative Planning.* Institute for Urban and Regional Planning. Long Beach, CA: California State University, IURD Working paper series.

Innovation Strategy – Helsinki Metropolitan Area (2006) Helsinki, Finland: Culminatum.

Isaksen, A. and Wiig Aslesen, H. (2001) "Oslo: In what way an innovative city?" *European Planning Studies*, 9:7, 871–87.

Johnson, S. (2002) *Emergence: The connected lives of ants, brains, cities, and software.* New York: Touchstone Book, Simon and Schuster.

Karlsen, J. and Larrea, M. (2012) "Emergence of shared leadership in situations of conflict: Mission impossible?". In Sotarauta, M., Horlings, I. and Liddle, J. (eds). *Leadership and Change in Sustainable Regional Development*. Abingdon, UK: Routledge.

Karppi, J. I. (1996) *Alueellistumisen ajasta toiminnan tiloihin: Yhteiskunnan institutionaalinen muutos ja organisaatioiden yhteistoiminta alueellisen kehittämisen resurssina.* Aluetieteen laitos, sarja A 17, Tampere, Finland: Strategisen yhteiskuntatutkimuksen seura ry ja Tampereen yliopisto.

Katz, B. and Bradley J. (2013) *The Metropolitan Revolution: How cities and metros are fixing our broken politics and fragile economy.* Washington, WA: Brookings Institution Press.

Kay, A. (2006) *The Dynamics of Public Policy: Theory and evidence.* Cheltenham, UK: Edward Elgar.

Kellerman, B. (2004) *Bad Leadership: What it is, how it happens, why it matters.* Boston. MA: Harvard Business School Press.

Kenis, P. and Schneider, V. (1991) "Policy networks and policy analysis: Scrutinizing a new analytical toolbox". In Marin, B. and Mayntz, R. (eds) *Policy Networks, Empirical Evidence And Theoretical Considerations* (pp. 25–59). Boulder, CO: Westview Press.

Kickert, W. J. M., Klijn, E.-H. and Koppenjan, J. F. M. (eds) (1997) *Managing Complex Networks: Strategies for the public sector.* London: Sage.

Kingdon, J. (1984) *Agendas, Alternatives and Public Policies.* New York: Longham.

Klijn, E.-H. (1996) "Analyzing and managing policy processes in complex networks", *Administration and Society*, 28:1, 90–119.

Klijn, E.-H. and Teisman, G. R. (1997) "Strategies and games in networks". In Kickert, W., Klijn, E.-H. and Koppenjan, J. (eds) *Managing Complex Networks. Strategies for the public sector* (pp. 98–118). London: Sage.

Komives, S. R. and Dugan, J. P. (2010) "Contemporary leadership theories". In Couto, R. A. (ed.) *Political and Civic Leadership: A reference handbook* (pp. 111–20). Thousand Oaks, CA: Sage.

Koppenjan, J. and Klijn, E.-H. (2004) *Managing Uncertainties in Networks: A network approach to problem solving and decision-making.* London: Routledge.

Kostiainen, J. (2002) *Urban Economic Policy in the Network Society.* Helsinki, Finland: Tekniikan akateemisten liitto.

Kostiainen, J. and Sotarauta, M. (2003) "Great leap or long march to knowledge economy: Institutions, actors and resources in the development of Tampere, Finland", *European Planning Studies*, 10:5, 415–38.

Kroehn, M., Maude, A. and Beer, A. (2010) "Leadership of place in the rural periphery: Lessons from Australia's agricultural margins", *Policy Studies*, 31:4, 491–504.

Kuhlmann, S. (2001) "Future governance of innovation policy in Europe: Three scenarios", *Research Policy*, 30, 953–76.

Lagendijk, A. (2007) "The accident of the region: A strategic relational perspective on the construction of the region's significance", *Regional Studies* 41:9, 1193–1208.

Lagendijk, A. and Oinas, P. (2005) *Proximity, Distance and Diversity: Issues on economic interaction and local development.* Farnham, UK: Ashgate.

Landry, C. (2006) *The Art of City-Making*, London, UK: Earthscan.

Leach, S. and Wilson, D. (2002) Rethinking local political leadership, *Public Adminis-tration*, 80:4, 665–89.

Lester, R. K. and Piore, M. J. (2004) *Innovation: The missing dimension*. Boston, MA: Harvard University Press.

Lewin, R. (1993) *Complexity: Life at the edge of chaos*, London: J. M. Dent.

Liddle, J. (2010) "The new public leadership challenge", *International Journal of Public Sector Management*, 24:1, 97–8.

Liddle, J. (2012) "Collaborative leadership in city-regions: Achieving social, economic, environmental objectives in partnership". In Sotarauta, M., Horlings, I. and Liddle, J. (eds) *Leadership and Change in Sustainable Regional Development*. (pp. 37–59). Abingdon, UK: Routledge.

Lindblom, C. E. (1959) "The science of 'muddling through'", *Public Administration Review*, 19:2, 79–88.

Linnamaa, R. (2002) "Development process of the ICT cluster in the Jyväskylä Urban Region". In Sotarauta, M. and Bruun, H. (eds) *Nordic Perspectives on Process-Based Regional Development Policy*. Stockholm: Nordregio Report 2002:3.

Linnamaa, R. (2004) *Verkostojen toimivuus ja alueen kilpailukyky* (Functionality of networks and regional competitiveness). Helsinki, Finland: HAUS kehittämiskeskus Oy.

Linnamaa, R. and Sotarauta, M. (2000) *Verkostojen utopia ja arki: Tutkimus Etelä-Pohjanmaan kehittäjäverkostosta*, (Utopia and every-day life of networks: The policy-network of South Ostrobothnia as a case in point). Tampere, Finland: Tampereen yliopisto.

Linnapuomi, P. (1990) *Kuntastrategiatyökirja* (Strategy workbook for local government). Helsinki, Finland: Suomen kaupunkiliitto.

Logan, J. and Molotch, H. (1987) *Urban Fortunes: The political economy of place*. London: University of California Press.

Lukes, S. (1986) "Introduction". In Lukes, S. (ed.) *Power: Readings in social and political theory*, 1–18. New York: New York University Press.

Lukes, S. (2005) *Power: A radical view* (2nd revised edn, first published 1974). Basingstoke, UK: Palgrave Macmillan.

Lysaght, M. J. and Reyes, J. (2001) "The growth of tissue engineering", *Tissue Engineering* 75, 485–93.

MacNeill, S. and Steiner, M. (2010) "Leadership of cluster policy: Lessons from the Austrian province of Styria", *Policy Studies*, 31:4, 441–55.

Madanipour, A. (2011) *Knowledge Economy and the City: Spaces of knowledge*. Abingdon, UK: Routledge.

Männistö, J. (2002) *Voluntaristinen alueellinen innovaatiojärjestelmä: Tapaustutkimus Oulun ict-klusterista*, [A voluntaristic regional innovation system: The ICT cluster in the Oulu area]. Rovaniemi: Lapin yliopisto.

Markussen, A. (1999) "Fuzzy concepts, scanty evidence, policy distance: The case for rigor and policy relevance in critical regional studies", *Regional Studies*, 33:9, 869–84.

Marsh, D. (1998) *Comparing Policy Networks*. Maidenhead, UK: Open University Press.

Marshall A., Finch D. and Urwin, C. (2006) *City Leadership: Giving city-regions the power to grow*. London: Centre for Cities.

Marshall, T. (2004) *Transforming Barcelona: The renewal of a European metropolis*. Abingdon, UK: Routledge.

Martin, R. and Sunley, P. (2006) "Path dependence and regional economic evolution", *Journal of Economic Geography*, 6:4, 395–437.

Martinez-Vela, C. A. and Viljamaa, K. (2004) *Becoming High-Tech: The reinvention of the mechanical engineering industry in Tampere, Finland*, MIT/IPC working paper 04-001. Cambridge, MA: MIT.

Meegan, R. (2012) "Leeds and national policy UK". In Parkinson, M., Meegan, R., Karecha, J., Evans, R., Jones, G., Sotarauta, M., Ruokolainen, O., Tosics, I., Gertheis, A., Tönko, A., Hegedüs, J., Illés, I. Lefèvre, C. and Hall, P., *Second Tier Cities and Territorial Development in Europe: Performance, policies and prospects – Scientific report*. The ESPON 2013 Programme, Applied Research. ESPON Coordination Unit and European Institute of Urban Affairs, Liverpool, UK: Liverpool John Moores University.

Meegan, R. (2015) "City profile – Leeds", *Cities*, 42: Part A, 42–53.

Mignerat, M. and Rivard, S. (2012) "The institutionalization of information system project management practices", *Information and Organization*, 22, 125–53.

Mintzberg, H. (1992) "Crafting strategy". In Quinn, J. B., Mintzberg, H. and James, R. M. (eds) *The Strategy Process: Concepts, contexts and cases* (pp. 105–13). New Jersey, NY: Prentice-Hall International.

Mintzberg, H. (1994) *The Rise and Fall of Strategic Planning: Reconceiving roles for planning, plans, planners*. New York: The Free Press.

Mintzberg, H. (2000) *The Rise and Fall of Strategic Planning: Reconceiving roles for planning, plans, planners* (2nd edn). New York: The Free Press.

Molotch, H. (1976) "The city as a growth machine: Toward a political economy of place", *American Journal of Sociology*, 82, 309–30.

Morgan, G. (1991) "Emerging waves and challenges: The need for new competencies and mindsets". In Henry, J. (ed.) *Creative Management* (pp. 283–93). London: Sage.

Nadig, R. R. (2009) "Stem cell therapy – hype or hope? A review", *Journal of Conservative Dentistry*, 12, 131–38.

Niiniluoto, I. (1989) *Informaatio, tieto ja yhteiskunta:* filosofinen analyysi. [Information, knowledge and society: philosophical analysis]. Helsinki, Finland: Valtion painatuskeskus.

Nonaka, I. and Konno, N. (1998) "The concept of 'Ba': Building a foundation for knowledge creation", *California Management Review*, 40:3, 40–54.

Normann, R. (2013) "Regional leadership: A systemic view", *Systemic Practice and Action Research*, 26:1 23–38

Northouse, P. G. (2007) *Leadership: Theory and Practice* (4th edn). Thousand Oaks, CA: Sage.

Padt, F. (2012) "Leadership and scale". In Sotarauta, M., Horlings, I. and Liddle, J. (eds) *Leadership and Change in Sustainable Regional Development* (pp. 60–79). Abingdon, UK: Routledge.

Paloheimo, H. and Wiberg, M. (2005) *Politiikan perusteet* (Politics) (3rd edn). Keuruu, Finland: Werner Söderström Osakeyhtiö (WSOY).

Pareja-Eastaway, M. (2009) "The Barcelona metropolitan region: From non-existence to fame", *Built Environment*, 35:2, 212–19.

Parkinson, M. (1990) "Leadership and regeneration in Liverpool: Confusion, confrontation or coalition?". In Judd, D. and Parkinson, M. (eds), *Leadership and Urban Regeneration*, (pp. 241–57). Newbury Park, CA: Sage.

Parkinson, M., Meegan, R., Karecha, J., Evans, R., Jones, G., Sotarauta, M., Ruokolainen, O., Tosics, I., Gertheis, A., Tönko, A., Hegedüs, J., Illés, I., Lefèvre, C. and Hall, P. (2012) *Second Tier Cities in Europe: In an age of austerity why invest beyond the capitals?* Liverpool, UK: Liverpool John Moores University.

Parsons, T. (1986) "Power and the social system". In Lukes, S. (ed.) *Power. Readings in social and political theory.* (pp. 94–143). New York: New York University Press.

Pelkonen, A. (2008) *The Finnish Competition State and Entrepreneurial Policies in the Helsinki Region.* Research Reports No. 254. University of Helsinki, Department of Sociology: Helsinki University Print.

Pelletier, K. L. (2010) "Leader toxicity: An empirical investigation of toxic behavior and rhetoric", *Leadership*, 6:4, 373–89.

Philo, C. and Parr, H. (2000) "Institutional geographies: Introductory remarks", *Geoforum*, 31:4, 513–21.

Pierre, J. (ed.) (2000) *Debating Governance: Authority, steering and democracy.* Oxford: Oxford University Press.

Powell, W. W. (1990) "Neither market nor hierarchy: Network forms of organization", *Research in Organizational Behavior*, 12:1, 295–336.

PX-Web Statfin Database, Statistics Finland. Available at: http://pxweb2.stat.fi/Database/StatFin/ (accessed 23 May 2015).

Rafiqui, P. S. (2009) "Evolving economic landscapes: Why new institutional economics matters for economic geography", *Journal of Economic Geography*, 9, 329–353

Rhodes, R. A. W. (2000) "Governance and public administration". In Pierre, J. (ed.) *Debating Governance: Authority, steering and democracy* (pp. 54–90). Oxford: Oxford University Press.

Riazi, A. M., Kwon, S. Y. and Stanford, W. L. (2009) "Stem cell sources for regenerative medicine", *Methods in Molecular Biology*, 482, 55–90.

Riggio, R. E., Chaleff, I. and Lipman-Blumen, J. (2008) *The Art of Followership: How great followers create great leaders and organizations.* San Francisco, CA: Jossey-Bass, A Wiley Imprint.

Rintala, H. (2006) *Koordinointi ilman hierarkia: Sopimuksellisuus ja verkostoituminen EPANET-verkostossa* [Coordination without hierarchy: Contacting and networking in the Epanet Network]. Vaasa: Hallintotieteen laitos, Vaasan yliopisto.

Ritvala, T. and Kleymann, B. (2012) "Scientists as midwives to cluster emergence: An institutional work framework", *Industry and Innovation*, 19, 477–97.

Riukulehto, S., Mäki, M. and Harjunpää, N. (2009) *Soihtu ja sateenvaro: Etelä-Pohjanmaan tutkimusverkosto 1999–2009* [Torch and umbrella: The research network of South Ostrobothnia 1999–2009]. Seinäjoki, Finland: Etelä-Pohjanmaan korkeakouluyhdistys.

Rodríguez-Pose, A. (1999) "Innovation prone and innovation averse societies: Economic performance in Europe", *Growth and Change*, 30, 75–105.

Rodríguez-Pose, A. (2013) "Do institutions matter for regional development?", *Regional Studies*, 47:7, 1034–1047.

Rodríguez-Pose, A. and Crescenzi, R, (2008) "Research and development, spillovers, innovation systems, and the genesis of regional growth in Europe", *Regional Studies*, 42:1, 51–67.

Russel, B. (1986) "The forms of power". In Lukes, S. (ed.) *Power: Readings in social and political theory*, (pp. 19–27). New York: New York University Press.

Rutten, R., Benneworth, P., Irawati, D. and Boekema, F. (2014) *The Social Dynamics of Innovation Networks.* Abingdon, UK: Routledge.

Rutten, R. and Boekema, F. (2012) "From learning region to learning in a socio-spatial context", *Regional Studies*, 46:8, 981–92.

Safford, S. (2004) *Searching for Silicon Valley in the Rust Belt: The evolution of knowledge networks in Akron and Rochester*, MIT/IPC working paper 04-002. Cambridge, MA: MIT.

Safford, S. (2009) *Why the Garden Club Couldn't Save Youngstown: The transformation of the Rust Belt.* Cambridge, MA: Harvard University Press.

150   *References*

Salmela, M. (1999) "Auringonlaskun maakunta" [The sunset region]. *Helsingin Sanomat*, 17 October 1999.

Samuels, R. (2003) *Machiavelli's Children: Leaders and their legacy in Italy and Japan.* Ithaca, NY: Cornell University Press.

Säntti, H. (2010) "Asenne ratkaisee, todistaa Seinäjoki" [It is the attitude that counts proves Seinäjoki], *Talouselämä*, 6 September 2010.

Scharpf, F. W. (1997) *Games Real Actors Play: Actor-centered institutionalism in policy research.* Boulder, CO: Westview Press.

Scott, A. (1988) "Flexible production systems and regional development: the rise of new industrial spaces in North America and Western Europe", *International Journal of Urban and Regional Research*, 12:2, 171–86.

Scott, W. R. (2001) *Institutions and Organizations* (2nd edn). Thousand Oaks, CA: Sage.

Senge, P. M. (1990) *The Fifth Discipline: The art and practice of the learning organization currency?* New York: Doubleday.

Simmie, J. (ed.) (2003) *Innovative Cities.* London: Spon Press.

Sotarauta, M. (1996) *Kohti epäselvyyden hallintaa: Pehmeä strategia 2000-luvun alun suunnittelun lähtökohtana* [Towards governance of ambiguity: soft strategy as a starting point for planning in the beginning of 2000]. Jyväskylä, Finland: Finn Publishers.

Sotarauta, M. (2005) "Shared leadership and dynamic capabilities in regional development". In Sagan and Halkier (eds.) *Regionalism Contested: Institution, society and governance.* Farnham, UK: Ashgate, Urban and Regional Planning and Development Series.

Sotarauta, M. (2009) "Power and influence tactics in the promotion of regional development: An empirical analysis of the work of Finnish regional development officers", *Geoforum* 40:5, 895–905.

Sotarauta, M. (2010) "Regional development and regional networks: The role of regional development officers in Finland", *European Urban and Regional Studies*, 17:4, 387–400.

Sotarauta, M. (2014) "Territorial knowledge leadership in policy networks: A peripheral region of South Ostrobothnia, Finland as a case in point". In Rutten, R., Benneworth, P., Irawati, D. and Boekema, F. (eds) *The Social Dynamics of Innovation Networks* (pp. 42–59). Abingdon, UK: Routledge.

Sotarauta, M. and Beer, A. (forthcoming) "Government, agency and place leadership: Lessons from a cross national analysis", *Regional Studies.*

Sotarauta, M. and Heinonen, T. (forthcoming) "The universities, innovation systems and human spare parts industry seen through a competence set: A conceptual discussion with and an illustrative case from Tampere, Finland".

Sotarauta, M., Horlings, L. and Liddle, M. (eds) (2012) *Leadership and Change in Sustainable Regional Development.* Abingdon, UK: Routledge.

Sotarauta, M. and Kosonen, K. (2004) "Strategic adaptation to the knowledge economy in less favoured regions: A South-Ostrobothnian university network as a case in point". In Cooke, P. and Piccaluga, A. (eds) *Regional Economies as Knowledge Laboratories.* Cheltenham, UK: Edward Elgar.

Sotarauta, M. and Lakso, T. (2000) *Muutoksen johtaminen ja luova jännite: Tutkimus Kainuun kehittämistoiminnasta* [Management of change and creative tension: A study of development work in Kainuu region]. Acta-sarja 132. Helsinki, Finland: Suomen Kuntaliitto.

Sotarauta, M. and Linnamaa, R. (1998) "The Finnish multi-level policy-making and the quality of local development policy process: The cases of Oulu and Seinänaapurit sub-regions", *European Planning Studies*, 6:5, 505–24.

Sotarauta, M. and Mustikkamäki, N. (2012) "Strategic leadership relay: How to keep a regional innovation journey in motion?" In Sotarauta, M., Horlings, I. and Liddle, J. (eds) *Leadership and Change in Sustainable Regional Development* (pp. 190–211). Abingdon, UK: Routledge.

Sotarauta, M. and Mustikkamäki, N. (2015) "Institutional entrepreneurship, power and knowledge in innovation systems: Institutionalization of regenerative medicine in Tampere, Finland", *Environment and Planning C: Government and Policy*, 33:2, 342–57.

Sotarauta, M. and Pulkkinen R.-L. (2011) "Institutional entrepreneurship for knowledge regions: In search of a fresh set of questions for regional innovation studies", *Environment and Planning C: Government and Policy*, 29:1, 96–112.

Sotarauta, M. and Saarivirta, T. (2012) "Strategy development in knowledge cities revisited: The roles of innovation strategy in Helsinki Metropolitan Area explored". In Garmann Johnsen, H. C. and Ennals, R. (eds) *Creating Collaborative Advantage: Innovation and knowledge creation in regional economies* (pp. 79–90). Farnham, UK: Gower.

Sotarauta, M. and Srinivas, S. (2006) "Co-evolutionary policy processes: Understanding innovative economies and future resilience", *Futures*, 38:3, 312–36.

Sotarauta, M., Kosonen, K. J. and Viljamaa, K. (2007) *Aluekehittäminen generatiivisena johtajuutena: 2000-luvun aluekehittäjän työnkuvaa ja kompetensseja etsimässä* [Promotion of regional development as generative leadership: In search of regional development officers of the 21st century and their competences]. Tampere, Finland: Tampereen yliopisto.

Sotarauta, M., Lakso, T. and Kurki, S. (1999) *Alueellisen osaamisympäristön vahvistaminen: Etelä-Pohjanmaan korkeakouluverkoston toimintamalli* [Strengthening the regional expertise milieu: An operational model for South Ostrobothnian HEI-network]. Tampere, Finland: University of Tampere.

Stimson, R., Stough, R. R. and Salazar, M. (2009) *Leadership and Institutions in Regional Endogenous Development*. Cheltenham, UK: Edward Elgar.

Stoker, G. (1997) "Regime theory and urban politics". In Judge, D., Stoker, G. and Wolman, H. (eds) *Theories of Urban Politics* (pp. 54–71). Thousand Oaks, CA: Sage.

Stoker, G. (2000) "Urban political science and the challenge of urban governance". In Pierre, J. (ed.) *Debating Governance: Authority, steering and democracy* (pp. 91–109). Oxford: Oxford University Press.

Stone, C. N. (1993) "Urban regimes and the capacity to govern: A political economy approach", *Journal of Urban Affairs*, 15:1, 1–28.

Storper, M. (2013) *Keys to the City: How economic, institutions, social interaction and politics shape development*. Oxford: Princeton University Press.

Stough, R. (2003) "Strategic management of places and policy", *Annals of Regional Science*, 37, 179–201.

Strambach, S. and Klement, B. (2012) "Cumulative and combinatorial micro-dynamics of knowledge: The role of space and place in knowledge integration", *European Planning Studies*, 20:11, 1843–1866.

Streeck, W. and Thelen, K. (2005) "Introduction: Institutional change in advanced political economies". In Streeck, W. and Thelen, K. (eds) *Beyond Continuity: Institutional change in advanced political economies* (pp. 1–39). Oxford: Oxford University Press.

Sydow, J., Lerch, F., Huxham, C. and Hibbert, P. (2011) "A silent cry for leadership: Organizing for leading (in) clusters", *The Leadership Quarterly*, 22, 328–43.

Termeer, C. J. A. M. and Koppenjan, J. F. M. (1997) "Managing perceptions in network". In Kickert, W. J. M. and Klijn, E.-H. and Koppenjan, J. F. M. (eds) *Managing Complex Networks: Strategies for public sector* (pp. 79–97). Thousand Oaks, CA: Sage.

Termeer, C. J. A. M. and Nooteboom, S. G. (2012) "Complexity leadership for sustainable regional innovations". In Sotarauta, M., Horlings, L. and Liddle, J. (eds) *Leadership and Change in Sustainable Regional Development* (pp. 234–51). Abingdon, UK: Routledge.

Tervo, H. (2002) *Rakkaudesta teknologiaan: Toimijaverkostonäkökulma Oulun IT-keskittymn rakentumiseen ja toimintaan* [For the love of technology: An actor network approach to the construction and development of the IT cluster in Oulu]. Rovaniemi, Finland: University of Lapland.

Tervo, H. (2005) "Regional policy lessons from Finland Regional disparities in small countries". In Felsenstein, D. and Portnov, B. A. (eds) *Regional Disparities in Small Countries*. Berlin: Springer-Verlag.

Tödtling, F., Asheim, B. and Boschma, R. (2013) "Knowledge sourcing, innovation and constructing advantage in regions of Europe", *European Urban and Regional Studies*, 20:2, 161–9.

Trickett, L. and Lee, P. (2010) "Leadership of 'subregional' places in the context of growth", *Policy Studies*, 31:4, 429–40.

Uhl-Bien, M. (2006) "Relational, collaborative and shared leadership theories approach leadership", *The Leadership Quarterly*, 17:6, 654–76.

Uhl-Bien, M., Marion, R. and McKelvey, B. (2007) "Complexity leadership theory: Shifting leadership from the industrial age to the knowledge era", *The Leadership Quarterly*, 18:4, 298–318.

Uyarra, E. (2010) "What is evolutionary about 'regional systems of innovation'? Implications for regional policy", *Journal of Evolutionary Economics*, 20, 115–37.

Valdaliso, J. M. and Wilson, J. R. (2015) *Strategies for Shaping Territorial Competitiveness*. Abingdon, UK: Routledge.

Vale, L. J. and Campanella, T. J. (2005) *The Resilient City: How modern cities recover from disaster*. Oxford: Oxford University Press.

Valtakari, M., Rajahonka, M. and Tikkanen, E. (2007) *Biomateriaaliosaamisesta liiketoimintaa. COMBIO-teknologiaohjelman loppuarviointi*. Teknologiaohjelmaraportti, Helsinki, Finland: Tekes.

Van de Ven, A., Polley, D. E., Garud, R. and Venkataraman S. (1999) *The Innovation Journey*. New York: Oxford University Press.

Vartiainen, P. (1998) *Suomalaisen aluepolitiikan kehitysvaiheita* (The phases of regional policy in Finland), Sisäasiainministeriö, aluekehitysosaston julkaisu, 6/1998. Helsinki, Finland: Ministry of the Interior.

Whittington, R. (1993) *What is Strategy – And does it matter?* Abingdon, UK: Routledge, Routledge Series in Analytical Management.

Witt, U. (2003) "Economic policy-making in evolutionary perspective", *Journal of Evolutionary Economics*, 13:2, 77–94.

Wrong, D. H. (1997) *Power: Its forms, bases, and uses*. New Brunswick, NJ: Transaction Publishers.

Yakhlef, A. (2010) "The three facets of knowledge: A critique of the practice-based learning theory", *Research Policy*, 39:1, 39–46.

Yigitcanlar, T., Velibeyoglu, K. and Baum, S. (eds) (2007) *Knowledge-Based Urban Development: Planning and applications in the information era*. New York: Idea Group Publishing.

Yukl, G. (1999) "An evaluation of conceptual weaknesses in transformational and charismatic leadership theories", *Leadership Quarterly* 10:2, 285–305.

Index

For Product Safety Concerns and Information please contact our EU
representative GPSR@taylorandfrancis.com
Taylor & Francis Verlag GmbH, Kaufingerstraße 24, 80331 München, Germany

www.ingramcontent.com/pod-product-compliance
Ingram Content Group UK Ltd.
Pitfield, Milton Keynes, MK11 3LW, UK
UKHW021848240425
457818UK00020B/773